TORN FISH

A Mother,
Her Autistic Son,
and Their Shared Humanity

Phyllis Mannan

For Helen,
Thank you for your
interest in my writing
and in my son.
Love,
Phyllis

TORN FISH

A Mother, Her Autistic Son, and Their Shared Humanity

Phyllis Mannan

Copyright 2015
Fairhaven Books

Cover design by Keri Knutson

ISBN-13: 978-0-9864022-0-3

Published in the United States of America

Portions of this book previously appeared in a somewhat different form: "Pot Roast Coming Around the Clock" in *A Cup of Comfort for Parents of Children with Autism* edited by Colleen Sell, Adams Media, 2007; "Wind Paper" in *RAIN Magazine,* Spring 2013; "The Torn Fish" in *North Coast Squid: A Journal of Local Writing,* 2013; and "The Real Thing" in *RAIN Magazine,* Spring 2014.

CONTENTS

CONTENTS

CONTENTS

CONTENTS

CONTENTS

V. AGES 37-41

VI. DAVID AT 43

For
Phil, David, Jon, and Lisa,
and for my mother,
Geraldine Meyers

AUTHOR'S NOTE

My purpose when I first started writing this book was to know, and understand, my son David, now forty-three; to get glimpses into his mind. As I wrote and shared my story, I realized I also wanted to explore what happens to relationships when the ability to communicate and understand feelings is severely limited.

In addition, I want to share what I've learned so others might gain insights into David's reality and learn from my experience. Each person with autism is different, but I offer a mother's perspective to help answer the questions: What is autism, and what happens when a child with autism grows up? Since observation is the only true test for the condition, personal experience provides the best knowledge. Finally, I hope to give David—and perhaps others with unique ways of thinking—a voice in the world.

David was born in 1971. At two-and-a-half years, he was diagnosed "developmentally delayed." The doctors who examined him at Oregon's Child Development and Rehabilitation Center explained he would probably not catch up with others his age. During a doctor's visit a few months later, I stole a look at his medical file and saw the words in bold type: "mentally retarded."

After David started special education classes, I observed other children with this label and realized its inadequacy. The words didn't explain his lack of eye contact, disinterest in other people, flapping, and echolalia (repetition of other people's words). When he was seven, I asked a teacher who had studied autism if she thought David had the condition. He had a few autistic traits, she agreed, but that didn't mean he was autistic. In 1978, the label was saved for children who spoke and interacted even less than David—the most severe cases.

At nineteen, when he was still in high school, David finally qualified for services from the Regional Program for Students with Autism, but his counselor was careful to say this didn't mean he was autistic. Our family doctor changed the classification on David's Special Olympics medical release form from "moderate retardation" to "autism." By then, a label meant little to me. It was a ticket to get services, nothing more. I knew each person was different and symptoms often overlapped.

As an adult, David expresses several typical autistic behaviors: limited eye contact; an aversion to touching others; echolalia; repetitive movements such as hand flapping and rocking; compulsive behavior like tearing paper and pushing down trash in garbage cans; a desire for sameness in the clothes he wears and the places he goes; the need to follow a rigid sequence of events; and the tendency to stay focused on one specific activity, such as pacing the house in a particular pattern. These behaviors increase with stress and decrease with calmness.

Our family's experiences mirror the change in how autism has been viewed since Dr. Leo Kanner first described it in 1943. For many years, the label applied only to persons with severe symptoms. Today, it's accepted that brain disorders like autism occur on a continuum. The new name, autism spectrum disorder (ASD), reflects this awareness.

When David was three, he tucked his hands into the bib of his overalls and smiled as if he felt secure. He loved to listen to books and records, strum a ukulele, and pound wooden pegs through a small board with a toy hammer. He uttered a deep, gleeful laugh when he heard "Silver Bells" on the record player and climbed on a chair to sing it for us. At eight years, he sang the ABC's with his grandmother as they climbed up and down her basement stairs. His happiness was contagious.

Though his delight in the world diminished during his teenage years and early adulthood, he remained calm and cheerful. But by the time he was twenty-two, he showed signs of increased anxiety and obsessive-compulsivity. With the aid of psychotropic medications and dependable routines, his symptoms improved. His late twenties and early thirties were mostly happy, in spite of the change to a different work program and the move to a group home.

By age thirty-eight, however, David had returned to the troubled behaviors of his early twenties: compulsive rituals; loud, repetitive talking; and pacing. When he was forty-one, our family helped him move to an adult foster care home. His turn-around, related in the book's final chapters, taught us important lessons about his needs.

When David lived with our family, he often slipped out the front door of our house to wait for his lift bus to take him to work before I had a chance to say goodbye. One morning, I opened the door and found him sitting on the porch step: A tall young man in a navy jacket and jeans, his black lunch box on the step beside him, he gazed at the street where his bus would appear. In the cool morning sun, vapor rose from David's head, still wet from his shower. This image of him sitting in the sun, haloed by particles of moisture, captures the mystery I've felt about what goes on inside his brain—a mystery that led me to write this book.

I.

Something white is wafted
by bubbles to the top
of the tank: a fish, splayed

at the spine, like two
fish, trying to swim apart,
thinly held by a tail.

1

The Torn Fish
Bound Together

At six-foot-three, David towered over the children in the waiting room of the pediatric dentist. He plucked Barney, a stuffed purple tyrannosaurus, from a chair, dropped him into the basket of toys in the corner, and sat down. Everywhere we went he straightened rooms, as if it was his job to organize the world's objects. The other mothers waiting with their small children glanced at him and went back to visiting. I suppose they'd figured out why at twenty-five he'd still be seeing a children's dentist.

Several colorful chains of toddler Legos lay abandoned in the center of the floor. My child—my man-child—sprawled on the green carpet next to them, his long body taking up most of the floor space. As the other mothers and I looked on, he unsnapped one bright blue, red, or yellow Lego after another until each plastic piece lay uncoupled. Then he put them in the basket. At home, he separated cassette tapes from their cases, crushed empty cans, and flattened cardboard boxes with the same fixed concentration. His need to disassemble objects mystified and, for some reason, embarrassed me.

I know now David's actions were a common trait of autism: restricted and repetitive behavior. The children who'd strung the Legos together had shown repetitive behavior, too, but their actions were less rigid. It was the restricted nature of the repetitions—their obsessive quality—that set David's actions apart. His behavior was similar to when he played with my hair spray can when he was three. I wanted to believe he was using his imagination when he danced a can on the countertop into the cabinet—that it was a person he was walking into a house or a car he was driving into a garage. But I realize now he moved the hair spray can the same way every day. The dancing motion wasn't a sign of imagination; it was a sign of autism.

Soon after David was diagnosed with a developmental delay at two-and-a-half years, I called the Oregon Dental Association to find a dentist in the Portland area who treated children with intellectual disabilities. They gave me the name of Lee Emery, whose office was then in a downtown Portland medical building. After the first visit, David slipped out the door of the crowded elevator on the wrong floor. The door closed behind him. I barely breathed until we got back to the floor where he'd gotten off. The door opened and there he stood, unharmed and unafraid. But the experience left me shaken. In the future, I was careful to grip his hand firmly in elevators.

A few years later, Dr. Emery had to pull four of

David's permanent teeth to prevent future crowding. Because of the anesthetic or because he'd swallowed too much blood, David vomited until late that night. For years afterward, he cried each time we took him to the dentist or the doctor, generalizing his experience. Nothing we said lessened his fear.

By the time our two younger children, Jon and Lisa, went to Dr. Emery, he'd moved his office to a Portland suburb. Dr. Emery saw them through braces. With regret, we'd decided the discomfort and care of braces would be too much for David. Jon and Lisa went to other dentists as they grew into adults, but David continued to see Dr. Emery until he moved to a group home at age thirty. I was grateful he had the opportunity to continue with a practitioner who knew and understood him.

The hygienist called David's name and he followed her into the adjoining room. I leafed through a travel magazine, wishing to escape. The other mothers and children were respectful, but David and I didn't fit in.

"Mommy, I found a torn fish!" A small boy, blond like David had been at his age, peered into the large fish tank next to the receptionist's window while his mother made his next appointment.

"Mommy, I found a torn fish!" He tugged on his mother's coat. She looked for her keys. He continued his mantra, but she took his hand and hurried him out the door.

Finally everyone left, even the receptionist. I bent

down over the tank, searching reefs and seaweed. It took me a few seconds to find what the boy had been talking about. Something white drifted at the top: a small fish, splayed at the spine, like two fish trying to swim apart, thinly held together by a tail. When the receptionist returned, I pointed out the creature, and she removed it with a small net.

The image of the torn fish stayed with me for days after we left the dentist's office. There was something profoundly sad about a dead fish floating on top of the water. When the fish was split down the center, the two parts still tied together, the sight was even sadder. In some way, I came to think David and I were like the torn fish, though we were alive and, most of the time, happy.

As I look back, our journey together has been long. At times, it's been dark and mapless, as all parents' journeys with their children are. Many have tried to help us, but we haven't had a guide. My husband, Phil, has been with us sometimes, but until recently he was working to support our family. When he wasn't consumed by work, his own need for separation sometimes kept him apart. He felt anguish over what he saw as our family's inability to prosper. By nature, he wants to fix problems, and David was one problem he couldn't fix. I've known other mothers of a disabled child with similar stories. It's not that the father doesn't love his child, but he finds it hard to relate. As a consequence, the mother becomes isolated from people outside the family, and, to some extent, from her husband.

No relationship can be reduced to a symbol, certainly not to the sad spectacle of a torn fish. But the bond between mother and child can be unyielding, especially if the child is disabled. Maybe this is why no matter how hard I try to write about David as a separate person, I find I'm writing about myself, too.

Phyllis Mannan

II.

After our son's birth
the doctors said,
He has a small white spot
on his right eye.
It won't cause a speck
of trouble—not a pebble
in his field.

Phyllis Mannan

2

The Small White Spot
David's Birth and Diagnosis

David was our first child. When we found out I was pregnant, we bought a house and fixed it up. I quit teaching, took a natural childbirth class and practiced my breathing. Following my doctor's instructions, I ate two eggs for breakfast each day and kept my weight gain to ten percent of my body weight. Some doctors had started allowing husbands in the delivery room. Not mine. I was relieved. I didn't want Phil to see me struggle giving birth.

We checked in at Portland's Good Samaritan Hospital in late March. After a nurse examined me and assured us the birth wasn't imminent, I urged Phil to pick up my new glasses at the optometrist's office. I couldn't wear contacts during the delivery, and I wouldn't be able to participate in the birth if I couldn't see the doctor, the nurses, and the baby. Getting new glasses was the last thing on my list of preparations. I wanted to do everything possible to follow the childbirth procedure I'd so diligently practiced.

The maternity floor was being renovated. In the

labor room, my pains were punctuated by hammering in the hallway.

A few hours later, the doctor explained the baby hadn't turned properly. He would give me medication to slow my contractions. The pain following the medication was excruciating. I wasn't able to use the breathing techniques I'd learned in my childbirth class.

The next day, David was delivered with forceps. I have little memory of his birth. A hospital picture shows a thin, groggy baby with red scrapes on his head and face. After the delivery, I lay in my hospital room floating—partly from pain medication, and partly from the euphoria women feel after they give birth. At twenty-seven, I'd done something miraculous: I'd delivered our first child, the first grandchild in both Phil's family and mine. With Phil, his parents and sister, my father and mother and sister and two brothers all gathered around me, the possibilities for our future seemed limitless.

The next morning, a nurse brought David into the room. "You are Mother . . . ?"

"Mannan."

"Here's Baby David." The nurse undressed him. He looked sleepy. I marveled at his small hands and feet. "Leave him wrapped in the blanket for feedings. You're bottle-feeding, right?" Breast-feeding was rare at that time. She would bring a bottle for me to feed David each morning and evening. Other times, he'd be fed in the nursery.

At each feeding, I'd gaze over at the two other

young mothers in my room, bottle-feeding their ravenous babies. David seemed uninterested in eating; in fact, he could hardly wake up. "Come on, my little leprechaun," the nurse would say, tapping him on the soles of his feet.

To make matters worse, Phil had a cold. During his visits, he sat across the room with a handkerchief tied over his nose. When I wasn't out of it because of the medication, I wondered how he felt. Was he sad about the scrapes on David's face? Was he worried about how thin David was? He didn't seem as happy as the other fathers who came to visit.

After the prescribed three days in the hospital, I was eager to leave. Phil arrived and we began to gather up my things and clothes for David.

"Mr. and Mrs. Mannan, may I speak to you?" An unfamiliar doctor appeared in the doorway, holding David. He explained he was the pediatrician on staff. "David has a small white spot on his right eye. You can hardly see it, and it won't affect his vision. I just wanted you to be aware of it."

The doctor handed David to me as I sat on the bed and Phil stood next to me. Looking closely at David's gray right eye, we *could* see a tiny fleck.

After the doctor left the room, I pulled a small cotton gown over David's head, threaded his arms carefully through the holes, and wrapped him in a green flannel receiving blanket my grandmother had embroidered with white scallops. As we left the hospital, Phil carried my overnight bag and a dozen yellow roses.

In subsequent weeks, sterilizing bottles and enlarging nipple holes for a baby who didn't eat much, we forgot about the spot on David's eye.

During the first year, David's physical development was in the low-to-normal range. He didn't sit up until ten months or babble like most of the babies we knew. Yet, we tried to reassure ourselves he was just slow getting started.

By the time David was sixteen months, I'd become more concerned about his development. He was walking but didn't look at other people or try to interact with them. If we tried to hug him, he pulled away. I could see worry on the faces of family members and friends.

Yet, at his regular check-up, David's pediatrician insisted our child was doing fine. As if to confirm this, he pointed out that David registered in the ninety-ninth percentile on the height chart. The doctor finished his exam and left abruptly, allowing no time for me to ask questions. I ran after him down the hall, but he walked into his office and closed the door behind him.

When I confided my anger and frustration to my friend Judy, she recommended her own children's pediatrician. At our first visit, the new doctor showed his concern. He asked to have David placed on the list for an all-day exam at CDRC, the Child Development and Rehabilitation Center. It would take at least a year to get an evaluation.

When David was two years and eight months, Phil dropped David and me off at CDRC, a large brick structure high above Portland on the campus of Oregon Health and Science University. Clinging to his daily schedule, Phil was on his way to work at our family's building specialty business. He would pick us up at the end of the day.

David, with his blond hair freshly washed, wore a new plaid corduroy suit with brass snaps I thought reflected how much we cared for him. Inside the building, he wanted only to run down the long hallway. I gripped his hand tightly. My other hand held a bag of diapers, extra clothes, and notes about David's development.

After registering, David and I migrated with an entourage of health professionals through the building. First, I sat on the floor with David on one side of a one-way mirror, trying to engage him in play with blocks and stuffed animals while others watched on the other side of the glass. I wished we were safely home in his bedroom with red, white, and blue striped wallpaper, playing with his blocks. But his strong hands were clapping; he was laughing. All seemed well—but I was afraid it wasn't.

An hour later, I stood in a small observation area with doctors and students who peered through the glass and wrote notes on clipboards. Inside the room, a speech therapist coaxed David to imitate sounds. David only babbled. "Touch your nose," the therapist said. David looked at a stuffed parrot on the floor.

Standing in the dark viewing area, I was struck by the power those around me wielded over our family's future. I felt I was being tested as a mother and was coming up lacking. David's new suit couldn't compensate for his lack of words. His ten "codes" tucked in my diaper bag included *ort* for orange juice, *toe* for toast, and *dub-e-dub-e-dub* for potato chip, but nothing for "mommy" or "daddy."

As the day wore on, David and I were less mother and son than objects of scientific research. We were caught up in a mysterious game in which I didn't understand the questions or the answers. A clinician measured David's head and posted its size on a sheet in the hallway like a grade. A social worker asked me, "Do you think there's anything seriously wrong with your son?" He seemed to be measuring how much truth I could take.

The day after the evaluation, Phil and I sat at CDRC, listening to doctors give reports.

"We think your son is developmentally delayed," one finally said.

"What does that mean?"

"We can't say exactly, but there will probably always be a gap between what he can do and what others his age can do." How big a gap? He couldn't say.

At home, I reasoned that a delayed airplane still arrives and decided the gap would be small. Phil didn't think there would be a gap. "They only gave us more questions," he shouted, his face red. "If you put a label on a child this young, it'll become a self-fulfilling prophecy." I could see his point.

During an appointment at CDRC a few months later, I sneaked a look at David's medical file when the doctor was out of the room. At the top it said, "Retarded Child."

Finally, I understood: David's life would be different from most children's; *our* life would be different. The tiny spot on David's eye was one of many signs that things had gone wrong early in my pregnancy. Knowing this truth was necessary for us to become good parents to David. Later, we would learn that "retardation" didn't adequately explain David's condition either.

But for now, the word was enough.

3

Buckling Down
Early Intervention

The weeks after David's diagnosis were like being lost in heavy fog. Phil and I struggled to comprehend that our first-born child would have difficulties his whole life. How could we help him? How could we deal with our situation? We felt alone and distraught. In desperate need of answers, I wrote to my friend, Lillian, a former teaching colleague and the only person I knew who had "a retarded child." Her daughter Peggy, an adult, lived on her own and worked at Goodwill. My friend's response came in a return letter: "David will teach you." A first-time parent, I couldn't imagine how he would teach us. I set her words aside.

Phil and I went over and over the test results and diagnosis, trying to decide what they meant. David's gross motor skills, such as walking and running, were normal. But his fine motor skills—his ability to string a bead or pick up a pebble—were at the one-year level. The most devastating numbers referenced his ability to use and understand language. At a little over two-and-a-half years, his communication skills were at the twelve to fourteen month level.

When David wanted something to eat, he took my hand and led me toward the kitchen. A tug in the direction of the sink or top shelf in the refrigerator meant, "I want water or juice." Raising my arm toward a cupboard shelf meant he wanted crackers. This "pull-language" would only work with those who knew him. Even then, it only worked to convey physical needs and wants. Would David ever say, "Look at that little yellow flower" and point into the garden?

He understood a few simple directions: "Let's go bye-bye," "It's time for lunch," "Don't do that." But he didn't understand—or didn't respond—when I said, "Come here," "Sit down," or "Take that to Daddy."

The doctors warned us David would probably not catch up with other children; there would always be a gap between what he could do and what others his age could do. The question was how big a gap. As a high school teacher, I assumed my child would attend regular school when he was five or six. For months, Phil and I went back and forth about whether I should sign David up for preschool. He would be three the following fall. Phil wanted to give preschool a try, but I could see David was far from ready.

The diagnosis "developmentally delayed" was soothing and seemed reversible. By sparing our feelings, the medical professionals who worked with us actually prolonged our adjustment. It would have been better if they had said they couldn't predict exactly what David's achievement level would be, but it was likely he would require special education and ongoing support.

Another question nagged at us: What had caused David's disability? Like most parents, we thought our child looked fine. But Dr. Chris Williams, the head pediatrician at CDRC, had pointed out David's ears were lower and more tilted than those of most people—rotated—and his facial features were slightly asymmetrical. And there was the tiny spot on his right eye we'd learned about after his birth. These could be signs of a chromosome abnormality.

When we mentioned David's unusual features to friends and family later, they seemed genuinely surprised. I'd noticed the asymmetry when I held him up to see his face in a mirror but dismissed it as unimportant. I'd never noticed his ears were lower and more tilted than most. If I had noticed, I wouldn't have considered the matter significant.

The pediatricians at CDRC felt certain something had happened early in my pregnancy—probably during the first six weeks—to cause these abnormalities and David's developmental delay. Perhaps a drug or a virus. I searched my mind. Had I unwittingly caused David's problems? I'd taken a lot of aspirin when I had severe abdominal pains about a month into the pregnancy, and I stained woodwork in the following months. If there were warnings in 1970 that these were risks to the fetus, I'd missed them.

David's doctors suggested he have two blood tests: one to rule out a chromosome disorder and the other to rule out the possibility that I'd contracted rubella during my pregnancy. I could have had the virus and not known it.

David and I transferred buses at the bottom of "Pill Hill," as locals called the site of the University of Oregon Medical School, now Oregon Health and Sciences University. We continued the circuitous route up the hill past the dental school, the bus letting people off at several stops, until we reached CDRC near the top.

In the doctor's office, a nurse searched David's wrists and arms, looking for a good vein to draw blood. He left and returned with a small straight jacket. I stood, terrified, as he laced it around David and inserted a needle into David's neck. David whimpered. Most toddlers would have howled.

Why had I allowed this—to satisfy our silly need for answers? We weren't being fair to David. Why hadn't the nurse warned me before he used a neck vein? I smoothed David's hair into place, wiped his nose, put on his clothes and we headed outside to wait for the bus.

When both the chromosome test and rubella test proved negative, Phil and I gave up trying to determine what had caused David's delay and tried to help him learn all he could. Until David entered preschool in the

Beaverton School District at three-and-a-half years, his training—and ours—came from CDRC.

After the evaluation, the first step was to choose toys to give David for Christmas that would increase his fine motor skills. Again, David and I rode the bus to CDRC, this time for an appointment with an occupational therapist. She noted David was interested in the physical aspects of toys and suggested we give him objects he could nest, squeeze, push, pull, or otherwise manipulate. I made a list: Nerf ball, paddle boat, music box Ferris wheel, Light Bright set, puzzles with seven to ten pieces, giant tinker toys, trucks and cars.

We should also look around the house for everyday objects to provide sensory experience. Listening to music, finger-painting, tearing paper, blowing soap bubbles and beating on a drum would be good activities, she noted. David was already doing most of these things. From an early age, he'd played with pots and pans and listened to books and records, too.

After Christmas, David and I began working with a young psychologist at CDRC, Dr. Pat Cotter. At the first visit, Pat said to observe David for fifteen minutes each day as he played, noting how long he stayed with each activity. Phil and I should constantly describe David's actions to him, without asking questions or giving commands. This was called "The Child's Game." It would establish good habits and help David associate his actions with language.

The Adult's Game, which followed, was harder. The goal was to have the child follow the adult's command. Using bits of candy as reinforcement, I would teach David to respond to the words, "Look at me." I knew learning to follow instructions was essential if David were to acquire other skills, but I was against using candy as a reinforcer.

The problem was I associated food rewards with animal training. Grappling with the news that David would not learn as other children did, I questioned a technique that made him appear less than human. Though candy was the most effective reward, I felt using it was demeaning to David. Later, I switched to bits of bacon, which seemed slightly more acceptable. I told myself I'd soon phase out the use of food entirely and use only pats and praise to teach him to obey.

The parent literature was strict: I was to work on only one behavior at a time. To teach the first command, "Look at me," I gave the same instruction for ten trials twice a day. If David made eye contact, I gave him a piece of lifesaver. Gradually, his eye contact improved.

The next command was "Come here." If David complied, I said, "Good, David, you came here" and gave him a piece of candy. If he didn't come, I said, "David, if you don't come here, you'll have to sit on the chair," a consequence called "time out." Sometimes I had to give a physical prompt to keep David in time out. I'd say, "David, sit in the chair," point to the chair and at the same time push downward on his shoulders so he had no choice but to sit. After he sat in the corner for three to five minutes, I'd give the command again: "Come here." It was important to be consistent until David complied.

One day in Pat Cotter's office, David got off the chair repeatedly. The room was hot, and David started to cry. Finally, Pat decided I would have to spank David—slap him twice on his bare bottom—to make him stay on the chair.

"I don't think he understands why he has to do this," I wailed.

"He has to learn to do as you say," Pat explained. "Otherwise, he won't be safe, and you won't be able to manage him when he gets older." I swallowed my objections and slapped David twice on his bare bottom when he got off the chair.

Though David was even-tempered by nature, teaching him to obey was tough. He often cried and left the designated area before his time was up, requiring another session on the chair. On sunny days, he'd drop to his knees in the driveway after a walk or car trip, refusing to come into the house. I'd ignore him as long as possible, hoping he'd come in on his own. Sometimes I went against the rules and offered him a snack if he came inside. But he often ended up in time out.

I was anxious to begin teaching David language, but Pat said a child must learn to obey basic commands and imitate sounds before he learns to speak. The process is sequential. Because David didn't imitate sounds or actions, I would have to teach this skill before I could teach language. Giving a command—*clap hands, hit the table, stand up, touch your nose*—I used ten trials and recorded the number of correct responses, as I'd done with the previous commands *look at me* and *come here*. David often had trouble when we switched from one action to another. If we'd been hitting the table and started to clap hands, he'd do both. When I finally did teach David names for familiar objects, he was more ready to learn than he would have been a few months earlier.

In the pattern of my parents' generation, I stayed home with David instead of returning to work after his birth. This was a benefit to me as well as to David. I became closely involved in my child's day-to-day training and received support from other mothers of young children in our neighborhood and at CDRC. Phil didn't have this advantage. He saw much of David's progress through my eyes and lacked the support I received. Though I tried to keep him up to date, he sometimes felt left out of the process. A parenting system in which the father shares in the child's daily activities benefits everyone, including the father.

4

Candling the Egg
Expectations

A psychologist once told me, "People who've had a happy childhood have the most trouble accepting adversity in adulthood." She might have been right, but a good start in life does help to provide a bulwark when bad things happen later. When I was growing up, my family had the usual worries—sickness, accidents, and financial shortfalls—yet my parents, grandparents, aunts and uncles surrounded me with love and pride in my accomplishments.

Phil had a happy childhood, too, and we tried to provide the same for our children. We took them to visit relatives to provide the sense of extended family we'd had. A family snapshot shows Phil and me holding David when he was a few months old, standing in front of a chicken coop in the sunlight, talking to my Aunt Hannah and Uncle Arthur. Phil's in a short-sleeved shirt and slacks and I'm wearing a pink sheath dress. I didn't date the photo, but it must have been the summer after David's birth, long before we knew about his disability.

Aunt Hannah and Uncle Arthur weren't our blood relatives, but there was no doubt they were part of our family when I was growing up near Scappoose, a small town twenty miles from Portland, Oregon. They celebrated birthdays, Thanksgivings, and Christmases with us, and we saw them almost every day. In my mind's eye, their weathered, two-story house under tall firs stands in perpetual shade, surrounded by sunlight.

In one memory, my younger brothers, Mark and Tim, walk next to me up the muddy, rutted driveway at the end of our gravel road. Our baby sister, Christine, has stayed home with Mother. We go around to the back of the house and smell sweet and sour cabbage and chicken simmering on the stove as we climb the porch steps.

Aunt Hannah, a short, stocky woman, stands scrubbing an egg with a wet, gray rag next to a table lined with wire baskets filled with eggs. Above her head, a fly strip dangles. Newspapers on the rough boards beneath her feet wear the yellow splotches of yolks from fallen eggs.

"Come in, come in, children." She places a clean egg in the wire basket, pins back the tail of her braid, and straightens the broad skirt of her house dress. "I'll get you a cookie." In the candling room off the porch, cookie tins keep company with crates of eggs. She returns, carrying a tin of butter cookies with walnuts, like the ones her family sold in their bakery in Germany.

When we finish the last crumbs, Tim says, "Can I

gather eggs?"

Aunt Hannah reaches for a garment hanging on the wall. "Wear my blue apron so the chickens will know you." The apron trails in the mud as Tim walks toward the chicken coop, swinging his basket. Uncle Arthur comes in from the field, a feed sack over his shoulders.

"Fah-tee, look who's here!" Fah-tee was Aunt Hannah's name for Uncle Arthur. I don't know what it meant—father maybe?

Uncle Arthur hangs his makeshift jacket on a nail and smiles at Mark and me. "Would you like to help me candle eggs?"

The candling room is cool and dark, like the root cellar. Uncle Arthur takes a washed egg from the wire basket and holds it against the light.

Mark peers up at him. "What are you looking for?"

"A spot. It means the egg's not fresh."

Mark frowns. "What kind of spot? If it has one, do we throw it out?"

Uncle Arthur looks at us without answering. He shows Mark how to place an egg against the light to be sure it's fresh. I'm older; I can wait. After Mark examines his egg, I hold one to the light. I can't see a spot, no matter how hard I look.

As a child, I didn't realize Aunt Hannah and Uncle Arthur's lives hadn't turned out the way they expected. Aunt Hannah thought she'd work in her family's bakery or keep house for her husband in Germany. In our country, she cleaned eggs with a dirty rag, made egg noodles and rolls yellow with yolks, and chopped heads off chickens. Uncle Arthur had been a banker; now he was a chicken farmer with impeccable handwriting who kept neat rows of numbers to record his egg sales. In the afternoons, he retired to his room to nap and read German books. He was the intellectual, Aunt Hannah the doer. As German immigrants, they'd been under close surveillance in our country during World War II. They loved children, but had none of their own—except us, the Meyers kids.

Their lives were like that of the candled eggs—uncertain. Phil's and my life would be like that, too.

5

My Fears as a Young Mother
The Toddler Years

In the 1970s, Phil and I often stayed with his parents at their beach cabin in Manzanita so we could work on the house we were building a few blocks away. When David was four, I spent five days alone with him in late August at my mother and father-in-laws' home. I wanted him to learn about the beach—to walk on the sand, sit on the driftwood, and smell the salt air. I wanted to learn more about him and myself and to learn about the place Phil and I had adopted as our second home.

After Phil left on Sunday to return to Portland, I began to question my decision. I didn't have a car or a telephone, and I didn't know anyone in town. What if David got hurt and needed a doctor? Less important but high on my list of anxieties, how would I monitor our social encounters alone: watch that David didn't take away another child's candy at the store, drink from a discarded cup, or enter into someone else's game on the beach? I wasn't sure how tough I should be in setting boundaries.

Thirty-one, and a first-time mother, I didn't know that much of his behavior was typical for a four-year-old. His loud repetitions, arm waving, and exaggerated gait drew attention. I didn't want others to think he was an unmanageable child who hadn't been taught good manners, and I didn't want to tell him to be quiet when this was his natural behavior. Beneath my qualms was a selfish fear: I didn't want our family to appear strange.

David was cranky after Phil left, but when he woke up from his nap, he seemed willing to meet me half-way. We were ready for adventure. I packed a picnic and we walked down Manzanita Avenue to the ocean in bright sunshine, David a few steps ahead of me.

At Ocean Road we crawled over large, uneven boulders to the wet sand and sat on a log overlooking the ocean. Neahkahnie Mountain, a large basalt headland, loomed to the north like a book end. David avoided the ham sandwich I'd packed but ate raisins and granola cookies. His eating habits frustrated me. He loved to have a sack of food to carry on trips or to eat while Phil and I worked on our property. But unless I intervened, he would eat sweet or salty snacks to the exclusion of healthy foods. Now that I've had two more children, this doesn't seem unusual.

After we ate, we played a game on the wet sand in which I tried to jump on David's shadow. He caught part of the idea but tried to jump on his own shadow instead of mine. I drew circles and squares on the wet sand and he tried to copy them. I wrote "David" and he tried to read the letters. Some were wrong, but he said his name after he spelled it. I was pleased he was learning words had meaning. We packed our things and climbed up the rocks.

We repeated this pattern each evening. On the last day, as we walked up Manzanita Avenue to go home, our shadows crossed and re-crossed. I thought of our closeness in the past week and in our lives. In spite of the growing influence of school in David's life, I would continue to play a large role.

I look back at the young mother I was with empathy and a little sadness. She was only starting to navigate the world with her son, and she was uncertain of herself. How would she get along for five days without her husband? Would other people think her son was strange and she an incompetent mother? I didn't realize then that most mothers want their children to behave well and reflect well on their family.

Journal entries from that week show David didn't get hurt and my fears about social encounters were mostly unfounded. At the grocery store, David wrenched free from my hand and ran headlong through the door, but no one seemed to care. When I got to him, he stood mesmerized in front of the candy rack. He chose a chocolate sucker—as any four-year-old might have done.

6

Running that Track Forever
The School Years

One day in his middle twenties, David said out of the blue, "Steph and Brook and Willa, they'll keep running that track forever." It took me a moment to realize he was talking about his teachers at Sunset High almost a decade earlier. During track and field practice for the Special Olympics state games each spring, they'd run alongside their students to encourage them. Apparently, David still saw them nurturing others, though Steph and Willa had retired. Did his mental snapshot of his teachers running beside him mean he wondered what had happened to them? Was it possible that he cared?

Twenty years earlier, David, five-years-old, uttered loud, happy gibberish as he circled our driveway with an exaggerated gait. His blond, Dutch boy hair flew in the bright September sun. He wore a red jacket and shiny Buster Brown shoes for his second day in a new class for children with speech and language delays at a school at the other end of our district. We lived in Garden Home, a suburb of Portland, in a close-knit neighborhood of sixty homes.

Several neighborhood children stood near me in our driveway, waiting for their bus to take them to the elementary school a mile away. The day before, Carolyn and Timmy had come to our house after school to wait for their mothers to get home from work.

The only child I didn't know was Natasha, whose family had moved into the neighborhood over the summer. She came and stood next to me, staring at David as he swooped around the driveway. "What's his name? . . . Where does he go to school?" She wasn't rude, simply curious, and David wasn't bothered by her questions. He continued his rounds.

I would take advantage of this as a teaching moment. "He's David. He's in a special class at Sunset Valley School."

Before I could go on, Natasha said, "I bet I know what kind of special class—one where the kids all talk like he does."

I didn't know how to describe the kids in David's class. Some had Down syndrome; some, like David, had autistic tendencies; some didn't make any sounds at all. My conversation with Natasha taught me the word "special" set kids apart. I should have said David was in a class where he could learn to talk. It's better to define a program by its purpose than to label it.

Carolyn, who lived across the street, shifted her school bag from one arm to the other. "When does David get home?"

"After you do . . . at quarter to three."

The children looked at me in disbelief. How could anyone as immature as David have a longer school day than they had? Actually, David's day was the same length as theirs, but his bus ride was longer.

A large yellow bus roared to the curb and the children—except David—climbed the steps. Looking back with a smile, Scott, a third-grader, had the last word: "But I'll bet he doesn't do math and cursive writing!" As David circled the driveway uttering sounds we couldn't understand, it didn't seem likely.

I'd begun to realize there was a whole "kid world" David wouldn't be part of. When Carolyn and Timmy had visited the day before, Timmy had bragged, "My class writes on second grade paper." Carolyn had announced, "My class writes on third grade paper." What kind of paper would David write on, if he learned to write at all?

As the years went by, David did learn to do math and cursive, though not at the same level as Scott, Timmy, and Carolyn. He finished school at Sunset Valley and went on to other self-contained classrooms at Beaver Acres Elementary and Five Oaks Junior High, mostly uninvolved emotionally with teachers and classmates. The short yellow bus that came for him in the morning and brought him home in the afternoon gave a sense of order to his world, and to ours.

In the end, it wasn't the intellectual gap, but the emotional one that most separated David from "regular kids," others in special ed, his teachers, and even those who loved him. Family photos show him holding Jon, born in 1978, and Lisa, born a year later, as if each were a bundle unattached to him in any way. His memory of high school teachers running the track beside him was unusual: It revealed a rare moment of caring.

Though David couldn't form close personal connections, he liked the familiar structure of school. He could count on things being more or less the same from day to day. Because he often had the same teacher and the same classmates for several years, his program stayed much the same from year to year, too.

David started school in 1974, the year before the Education for All Handicapped Children Act passed, but our district already provided special education beginning at three years of age. The Individuals with Disabilities Education Act (IDEA) later required states, in order to receive federal funds, to provide special education consistent with federal standards for all students. In a landmark statement, IDEA entitled every student to "a free and appropriate public education in the least restrictive environment." A team of professionals from the school would meet with the parents of each special education student to identify his or her educational needs and to develop annual goals. The goals would be recorded in an Individual Education Plan (IEP). The IEP provided a roadmap and a way to gage progress. [1]

One thing that bothered me during David's school years was the way educational labels seemed to define him and to set limits on his abilities. When he entered school at three years of age, he was placed in a Trainable Mentally Retarded (TMR) class because his IQ fell below 50. If it had been above 50, he would have been in an Educable Mentally Retarded (EMR) program. The TMR label followed David through elementary school and junior high. We never questioned the validity of his placement because the classroom curriculum seemed appropriate. But the arbitrary cut-off meant some children weren't properly placed and parents had to argue their case. Children don't fit neatly into categories, and IQ tests are notoriously inaccurate when applied to children with limited communication skills. The labels "trainable" and "educable" revealed prejudice, too. Who's to say a child isn't educable?

Educational labels improved by the time David entered high school, where his classroom was called the Independent Skills Center. Evidently, someone realized it was better to label a program according to what it was intended to do, improve students' skills, rather than to label the people in it.

The biggest problem with the word "retarded" was its use as an intellectual slur. David couldn't tell me the names he was called, but I saw other special education students deemed retarded by the general student body and even by their friends who were cognitively impaired themselves. Many wrote or spoke about how much this hurt them. My teaching years were filled with students calling one another "retard" or saying "That's retarded" if someone tripped or dropped a pencil. Even high school advanced placement students used intellectual slurs freely. Each time I heard "Retard!" in a classroom or a hallway, I stood up for David and other children with differences: "I won't allow put-downs."

I once had a dream in which a man in a white coat peered across a large desk at me. "Didn't you *know* you're retarded?" My face flushed. I began to sweat. I felt sick to my stomach. *No, no!* Waves of humiliation engulfed me. If the sentence the white-coated man in my dream delivered had been real, I would have questioned my abilities. I would have let others do things for me because they could do them better or faster. I would have quit trying. The label would have altered my internal expectations.

Few labels are acceptable to the people who bear them. Even official labels hurt. Self-advocates who have intellectual disabilities say they simply want to be called by their given names: Brian, Jason, or Sally.

Though David must have received taunts in junior high and high school, he didn't seem to feel hurt or to lose self-esteem. This seems impossible when I consider the trauma most teenagers go through in relating to their peers. David's inability to understand social cues may have protected him from being hurt. Maybe he didn't realize what his fellow students thought of him. More likely, he sensed their feelings and, already a loner, kept his distance.

As a nation and a culture, we're moving in the right direction by saying "a person with an intellectual disability," or "a person with autism," labeling the condition rather than the person. Even the term "mentally retarded," which referred to anyone with an IQ of 70 or less, was an improvement over previous labels such as "idiot," "brain damaged," and "feeble-minded." But this term, too, has been replaced in the ongoing search for a name that has no stigma. The preferred expression now is to say that the person has "an intellectual disability," defined as a condition with significant limitations in intellectual function and adaptive behavior that originates before age eighteen.[2]

It's possible, though, to go too far in trying to be politically correct. Recently, I heard the term "people with developmental differences" used in place of "people with developmental disabilities." I like the distinction, but the term only works if the differences are minor, as in some cases of Asperger's Syndrome or high-functioning autism. Truth must trump political correctness. David's bus pass used to bear the words "Honored Citizen" because disabled riders were categorized with Senior Citizens. This was ludicrous. As a society, we need to learn that imperfection is okay instead of trying to cover it up.

As I explained in this book's introductory notes, David was never formally diagnosed with autism. At nineteen, he was accepted for services from the Regional Program for Students with Autism. The next year his doctor changed the name of his condition on his medical records from mental retardation to autism. This reflected a widening in the definition of autism and the understanding that traits occur across a spectrum. The current definition of autism and autism spectrum disorder (ASD) is that it is "characterized, in varying degrees, by difficulties in social interaction, verbal and nonverbal communication, and repetitive behaviors."[3]

For many years, I wasn't comfortable with David's new "diagnosis." Autism was too trendy, too nebulous. How could David be lumped in the same category with Temple Grandin, a gifted animal scientist who had designed one-third of the livestock-handling facilities in the country? I was wary autism was another euphemism like "mentally challenged." I'd spent nineteen years getting used to the term mental retardation and wasn't going to give it up easily. But the more I read about autism, including Grandin's books, I saw how David fit the definition. I especially liked the idea that the condition occurred on a spectrum. Core traits, such as impairments in communication and socialization, were the same, but the degree varied. This made sense. Didn't all human traits fall on a spectrum?

Still, I struggled with the label's vagueness. The term Autism Spectrum Disorder did nothing to explain the word "autism" itself. Who were the people on the spectrum? I found that some had mild perceptual symptoms, others the severe problems of classic autism discovered by Leo Kanner. Many, like David, had formerly been labeled "retarded." Forty to fifty percent had no intellectual impairment at all. How could the word mean anything when it was so encompassing?

If I told someone my son was autistic, the person had no mental picture of what that meant. Was he verbal? Did he rock back and forth? Was he completely closed off from the world? Was he savant, like Rain Man? Could he read? I needed to add information to the label, to flesh it out. After years of people nodding when I said my son was retarded, now I had to explain. The biggest surprise was that, with this new label, negative associations were replaced with interest and curiosity. Yet, David hadn't changed. This change in people's attitudes demonstrates a problem with labels: Not only are they hurtful, but they're often inaccurate.

When David said, "Steph and Brook and Willa, they'll keep running that track forever," he wasn't concerned about educational or societal labels; he was remembering a time his teachers ran along beside him, encouraging him. His comment reminded me of the enormous role his teachers played in his life—and how far he had come.

7

Ghosts at Tryon Creek
Sensory Perception and Self-Awareness

One spring day, I sorted through a box of David's Sunset High School papers. First, I opened a booklet with metal fasteners titled "David's Book." Inside were the text and sketches from a field trip to Tryon Creek, a local woodland park, by students in his Independent Skills Center class. On one page, David had drawn a succession of ghost-like figures with two dots for eyes, one dot for a nose, and a cheerful grin, but no ears or hair.

A caption by a teacher or assistant tells the reader these figures are David and his classmates walking on a trail. Six of them with oval feet perch, like birds on a wire, in the upper half of the page. Four others without feet, or a trail, float below. Each figure has a name printed in David's writing vertically on its torso: Kevin, Heidi, Anna, Melissa, David, and five other names I can't make out.

David may have simply drawn his classmates to the best of his ability, as others use stick figures to represent people. Or, an aide may have suggested he draw sack-like bodies so he would have room to write names on them; I'm never certain how much help he had with his literacy projects. Yet, there's something eerie in these sexless ghosts. Something autistic. They smile, but they look closed off from one another and the world. Without arms and legs, they appear unable to move. And if they're walking on a trail at Tryon Creek, why are there no trees, no creek? I think how often I've pointed out a sparkling scene in nature only to have David look away. And why has he so often referred to himself as *you* or *he?* Is this a linguistic problem, the result of echoing others' speech, or does he lack the sense of self most people take for granted? Is his picture a sign of a distorted view of himself and others?

I'd been troubled by David's tearing the edges of pictures of people when he was younger. I once opened a photo album of our family's trip to Disneyland to find Goofy with his hat and jacket tattered. Mickey stood with notched ears, waving at visitors, his white glove missing a thumb. Strangely, David had torn the edges of the characters he seemed to like best. He notched pictures of friends and family members the same way. Did his tearing mimic the way memory works, or did it reflect the way he saw people?

I flipped through another booklet from David's school years titled "My Favorite Things." A young man with humongous arms and three large, claw-like fingers on each hand smiled at me from the page. In contrast to the figures in the earlier picture, this person had arms and legs, hair, and recognizable clothing. The large blocks of red and black across his chest and black pants reminded me of the red and black sweatshirt and black jeans David wore at seventeen.

David's favorite things appear to have been activities. On the cover, someone stretches out on a narrow bed similar to his long-boy twin. On the page titled "My Favorite Sport," a smiling green figure dribbles a basketball. "My Favorite Music" is illustrated by a man playing what looks like a guitar.

But the most surprising page is the last: A cheerful-looking woman in a purple dress is captioned, "Best friend is Grandma. Grandma is neat. She has pretty brown hair." The woman's spider-thin legs and brown clodhopper shoes may be off, but David captures a bit of my mother's generous spirit. As I look at his child-like drawing, I wonder how many high school students list their grandmother as their best friend.

A teacher's note inside the cover explains students dictated the text to an assistant, who wrote the captions. Then they drew a picture to match their words. Sometimes they had to redraw the picture several times. The self-portrait was the hardest. Aides had to hold up a mirror to help students see what they looked like. I can only imagine how hard this must have been for the assistants and teachers, all of whom went to great lengths to help David and other students develop a better sense of themselves and those around them.

A third article in the box was a journal entry dated June 1989, when David was eighteen. Written in pencil, in large, cryptic letters on notebook paper, it provides a rare glimpse into his thoughts:

> *today fel ok*
> *i can't breathe*
> *my ears hurt*
> *I bat basball*

Again, I don't know how much help David had when he wrote this log; an assistant may have coached him. Though the misspelled words *feel* and *baseball* suggest he wrote the entry himself, he would have needed help to spell *breathe* correctly. And I doubt he would have written how he felt without a prompt. Yet, there are particles of truth to the journal entry. In June, David's hay fever often made breathing difficult. His narrow ear canals filled with fluid. We didn't realize his discomfort unless we saw him pull on his ears.

It was characteristic that, in spite of these physical problems, David said he felt okay and had batted a baseball. We all have trouble identifying what's wrong with us sometimes, but David finds this harder than most. During a recent spell of vertigo, my mother laughed and said, "It's not me being dizzy; it's the house going around." David might not realize his perceptions are at fault when things seem out of sync; he might think the world itself is distorted.

At its most basic level, life consists of what comes to us through our senses. When I grasp a prickly weed with bare fingers, smell cedar bark, watch an ant scurry across warm deck boards, hear an owl's *whoo* or taste a tart apple, I assume my experience is the same as everyone else's. But even among people with typical brain function, each person's experience will be a little different.

People with autism often have abnormally strong or weak responses to some senses.[4] David is hypersensitive to touch. As a baby, he stiffened and drew away when held. Even as an adult, he shrinks back if hugged but will give a half-hearted embrace if someone says, "Would you like to give me a hug?" He needs to control the pressure against his body. This "standoffishness" can make him seem aloof, even if one understands his reaction is beyond his control.

As a teenager, he found new ways to deal with his sensitivity to touch. If I forgot to cut the manufacturer's tag from inside his shirt collar, he tore the tag off, leaving a gaping hole. He ripped the insignia, with its rough under-side, from polo shirts before I bought ones without a logo, ripped the innersoles out of his shoes and flushed them down the toilet, cut up new jeans and flushed them too. Anything that chafed his skin was fair game. The plumber laughed, but we groaned when we got the bills. David communicated what he needed without words. As he's grown into adulthood, he's been more tolerant of clothing tags and innersoles. But we make certain his new shirts don't have an emblem on the front.

In spite of his aversion to being touched, David sometimes uses touch to navigate and understand personal interactions. When he lived with the family, he liked to grocery shop with me and help to put the groceries away. As we maneuvered around our small kitchen island one day, he bumped my leg. "Sorry, you're in your way," he said, confusing the pronouns. In a familiar gesture, he bent down and touched the place on my calf he thought he'd hurt, as if to locate the pain. Then he pressed the spot, perhaps to restore it or to set things right. His action reminded me of how I smoothed my children's foreheads when they were sick. It seemed to show empathy.

In a later chapter, I describe how David once touched my head as if to locate where memories originate. Again, he seemed to be trying to make the abstract into something he could grasp. His desire to understand apparently overcame his unwillingness to touch another person.

When David was fourteen, he talked at Easter about the holes in Jesus' hands and rubbed his own hands. The holes appeared to be the only part of the passion story he understood. Years later, when we talked about Good Friday, he said, "Yeah, good Friday and better Friday." Along with singing and listening to music, touch seems the most effective way for him to understand spiritual concepts and to express his faith.

Sometimes, David uses touch to understand objects in the environment, too. Since he was twelve, our family has vacationed in Sunriver, a Central Oregon resort with a large network of bike trails. We hoped our family could bicycle together, but David would need to learn to ride a bike. We rigged an adult-size bicycle with training wheels so he could practice riding in a school parking lot near our home in Portland, but, try as he might, he couldn't acquire the necessary balance even with training wheels. Our solution was for Jon and Lisa to ride bikes with Phil, and for David to walk the trails with me.

Sunlight cast shadows through the pine trees and bitterbrush. Six-foot three inches, with long legs, David walked fast.

"Wait!" I called when he strode too far ahead.

He stopped near a yellow yield sign where a street intersected our path. As I approached, he touched the sign lightly. I'd seen this action before, when he fingered a book cover he couldn't comprehend or thumbed through a photo album of old snapshots, trying to make out the place and time. He seemed to hope touch could give him the information he needed.

"Stop?" He looked at me, his hand on the yield sign.

"Yes." Close enough. I thought of people who use touch to replace seeing and of children with learning disabilities who read by feeling letters made of sandpaper. One sense compensates for another. Touch sometimes bothers David, but it also gives him valuable information to help him understand his world.

David shows hypersensitivity not only to touch, but also to loud sounds. When he was four, we went to the beach for a Fourth of July fireworks display. After the first loud boom, he began to cry. When we couldn't console him, Phil carried him to his grandparents' house a few blocks away. His fear of dogs, too, seems related to their barking. When he was eight, we moved to a house with a narrow side yard, where we could hear a neighbor's dog barking behind the fence. The move itself was traumatic for David, who requires sameness for stability, but the barking prolonged his adjustment to a new home.

It's harder to determine David's sensitivity to visual input than to touch and hearing. According to recent studies, some people with autism have a hypersensitivity to brightness or brightly colored patterns, have trouble organizing the parts of a scene into a cohesive whole, and have a lack of coordination between messages sent from the eyes and ears to the brain. A scene might appear like a movie in which the sound track is out of sync with the picture.[4] In this case, I hope the research doesn't apply to David's experience.

We don't know about David's sense of smell, but I suspect it's weak since he never describes a smell or responds to strong odors. Because he talks about "good food" and shows preferences for one food over another, I think his sense of taste is normal.

There are also other senses we seldom think about. David has a high tolerance to warmth and cold. Because he finds it hard to change his clothing habits, he wears a heavy jacket well into spring or summer and a short-sleeved shirt into fall and winter, but he never seems bothered by his choices. If someone urges him to change to something more fitted to the weather, he says, "I'm fine."

He also seems to have a high tolerance to pain. Headaches, toothaches, stomachaches, sunburns, colds, flu—he seems oblivious to all. Perhaps a high pain tolerance is compensation for other senses being heightened, but unreported pain can lead to physical problems getting worse. For this reason, it's considered a risk factor in David's support plan.

David's sense of body awareness seems distorted, too. When he walks through a crowd, he almost grazes the people he passes. I'm amazed he doesn't step on someone's toes or knock them down. Yet, he never touches anyone; he seems guided by uncanny radar. His actions probably reflect a lack of social awareness. If he had a normal perception of personal space, he wouldn't move so close.

The last "sense" we often take for granted is our sense of self. Though I was afraid David would never be capable of self-reflection, I was reassured by Richard Restak's assertion in *The Brain Has a Mind of Its Own* that much knowing goes on below the level of conscious awareness.

A practicing neurologist, Restak writes, "Perception, recognition, memory—all three processes are embedded within the brain via a hierarchical scheme. Failure at the highest level (conscious awareness—knowing what one knows) doesn't mean the absence of knowledge." He cites intuition, hunches, reading others' body movements, and riding a bike as examples of knowing without conscious awareness. [5]

Though David knows things he can't express, it appears his sense of self has been compromised. Scientists have devised experiments to learn how self-awareness develops in humans and why it's altered in people with disorders like schizophrenia and autism. They now believe emotions play an essential role in helping us understand the world, others, and ourselves. In autism, the ability to express and understand emotions has been disrupted.

Writing about her son with autism in *The Boy Who Loved Windows*, Patricia Stacey explains, "As a child is developing, everything he does and thinks is largely because of his emotions. . . . The emotions allow a child and an adult to sort material. Knowledge, wisdom, experience, information: Each of these is brought into complex networks in the brain, into endless and surprising categories, all finding their place in the emotions, which compose the human ability to ascribe meaning."[6]

Though autism makes self-awareness difficult, I began to notice a pattern in David's echolalia and self-talk during his twenties: Its purpose was often to self-monitor, the same purpose I saw in my own interior monologues. Clipping shrubs that didn't need pruning, David asked himself, "Why do you want to do that?" He answered his question, "No reason." Pacing from room to room, he said, "Don't have time to walk around. Quit the walking around. I don't like it."

During an ice storm, he told himself as he inched his way up our dangerous hill, "Walk on the bark dust, not the slippery, falling-down ice."

Other times, the purpose of his self-talk was self-consolation or self-encouragement. As four trees in our yard plummeted in a wind storm, he pleaded, "The trees won't fall down." When the workmen came to cut them into firewood, he consoled himself, "Don't worry; they won't cut the trees, they won't." In the middle of a severe self-scolding, he said, "You're doing the best you can," words I'd told him since he was a toddler.

In spite of his difficulty reading and expressing his emotions and those of others, David has a sense of right and wrong. "I'll learn, I'll do the right thing," he tells me after he shuffles through the paperwork in our office, placing things where Phil and I will have to find them. "I'm sorry," he says when he refuses to wear clean clothes because he wants to wear the same ones every day.

In his self-talk, I see encouraging confirmation of our common humanity. He continues to impress me with his insistence on self in spite of his disability. Each act and feeling brings him closer to self-actualization. He learns who he is through his experiences.

Because of these characteristics, I'm convinced the underlying principles that make up a self are the same for everyone. Autism may impair thinking, feeling, communicating, and the ability to relate to other people, but it does not preclude personhood.

Still, perhaps it was not a coincidence David drew himself, and his classmates, as ghosts. His communication booklet about his favorite things and his journal entry, as well as my experience and the current research, tell me a sense of self depends upon a clear relationship to the outer world. We abstract from our experience. If our sensory world is damaged, we lack a clear connection between our feelings, actions, and ideas. We lack a clear understanding of ourselves.

8

The Purple Gown
The Transition from School to Work

I awoke with anticipation and dread, white sheets tucked around my neck like a protective cloak. David was twenty-one, the maximum age for receiving public education in Oregon. He would graduate that afternoon in a small ceremony in his classroom at Sunset High. For eighteen years, a short yellow school bus had picked him up and dropped him off at our house. In three days, this would change. He would board a Tri-Met lift bus in front of our house to travel to Tualatin Valley Workshop, to package wires and other small components for Intel. Though he'd spent part of each school day at the workshop the past few months, we had no way of knowing how he would respond to daily work without the support of school staff.

David could have attended Sunset's regular graduation, but the only students he knew outside his special education circle were peer tutors who came to his room to work one-on-one with him and P.E. buddies who encouraged him to do his best in the gym or on the track. Though some of his special ed classmates had formed close bonds with those outside their classroom, David had not. He hadn't been mainstreamed since grade school, when he'd been part of a regular music class for a short time. For the past eight years, his school life had been relegated to his self-contained classroom, and washing windows and sweeping floors around the building. The nondisabled students in his graduating class moved in a parallel, but different, universe. He would not have felt part of the regular graduation ceremony. So, when a notice had arrived a few weeks before, asking whether David would take part in the school graduation or the one in his classroom, I hadn't hesitated to check "classroom."

Phil and I walked with my parents down a long hall at the end of the sprawling, one-level building. David's classroom was far from the hub of the school, where it was convenient for staff to escort students to their buses and for drivers to drop them off. It was also near the cafeteria, where students in David's program worked to count milk and juice cartons, clean tables, and sweep floors. They needed to learn marketable skills, but I worried that serving and cleaning up after their fellow classmates made them second-class citizens. The location of the room also emphasized students' separation from the rest of their school.

Inside the classroom twenty-six students, three teachers, a host of assistants, and a few family members milled about. Tables were pushed to the side and chairs set up in rows. Students who weren't graduating would sit in the audience. Seven graduates, some in wheelchairs, sat in their gowns at the front of the classroom. As in the regular ceremony, boys wore purple gowns, girls white—Sunset's school colors. An assistant straightened hats and tassels. Some graduates seemed proud of their garb, but David stared ahead, as if unaware this was an important marker in his life. If he wasn't emotionally involved in his own graduation, how were we to feel excited?

I sat down and whispered to Jimmy's mother, in the row ahead, how handsome her son looked in his purple gown. She murmured back that David looked handsome, too.

The short program began. The vice-principal congratulated the graduates on their years of hard work and wished them well. He called each graduate's name and handed him or her a modified diploma. They had satisfied the requirements laid out in their Individual Education Plans. They had met an important goal. But David showed no sign he understood his achievement, no pride in his eighteen years of public education.

After the mini-program—more like a family birthday party than a public event—a large sheet cake was cut on the maple table in the kitchen where students had eaten pizza or macaroni and cheese they'd made in their cooking class.

My parents took us to a Shari's restaurant for lunch. As we sat in a large red booth by the door, David ate a hamburger without looking at any of us. I perused the cards from his teachers and county services coordinator. One, signed by his fellow classmates, had clouds and a rainbow on the front. The inscription read, "Whatever you do, may luck be with you." He would need luck—and maybe a guardian angel. Some names on the card were written in a large, childish hand, others evidently printed by an aide for someone unable to sign his or her own name. Michele had written "I'll see you." Maybe she was right. David would attend Special Olympics events, as well as day trips, dances, and game nights offered by the Park and Recreation District.

David's graduation made me realize how much his aloneness had seeped into my psyche, as it had worked its way into the life of everyone else in our family. In his early primary grades, I'd joined "the mom's group," an informal organization of mothers who had kids in special education in our school district. Most of us met at The Washington County Arc, at that time called The Association for Retarded Citizens. Together with our husbands, we served on the Board and helped to rehabilitate the building. In the beginning, we held our mothers' meetings in a local church. After our children were in school, we went out to lunch once a month and shared stories over soup, salad, or a sandwich. I found strength in knowing others were going through similar struggles.

But by the time David was in high school, the other moms, many of whose children had Down syndrome, were talking about dances, sleepovers, and boy-girl relationships. Although their children didn't fit in with "the normal kids," they fit in with each other.

David had no interest in making friends and no skills that would have helped him if he had. If he went to a dance, he danced alone. If a classmate called him, he hung up. It was hard to stand by and watch him ignore those who cared about him, to see them turn away because they felt rebuffed.

The other moms in our group continued to invite me to their meetings, but I started to make excuses for why I couldn't attend. Before, I'd thought they could understand our family in a way no one else could. Now, I felt a separation. David hadn't changed; I'd simply become more aware of his differentness.

By the time David began to receive services from the Regional Program for Students with Autism at nineteen, his patterns—and our family's—had been set. Even if he had been diagnosed with autism earlier, there were few support groups for families at that time. Parents joined groups like The Arc and the Moms' Group. But not many parents in these groups had a child with autism. If they did, the child hadn't been identified as autistic, but rather lumped in with the "mentally retarded" population. As a result, many families, like ours, went without the support they needed.

In spite of my apprehension on the day of David's graduation, he settled in well at Tualatin Valley Workshop. He continued the routines he'd learned his last year of high school. Though he developed anxiety in future years that hindered his happiness and performance, the transition from school to work was almost seamless.

A small, plastic replica of a young man in a purple graduation gown still stands on top of David's bookcase. I don't know whether he keeps the object there because it means something to him or because he's grown used to having it in that place. But the tall, slender young man in a purple gown looks much the way David did at twenty-one.

Phyllis Mannan

III.

We'll stop the wind, he says.
The trees won't fall down,
they won't.

The ones that already fell?
I ask.
Yes, he says.

Phyllis Mannan

9

What Are People For?
Problems Relating to Others

"Mom is home. Plug the radio in. Put the new Dodge Caravan truck back in the garage," David's voice boomed in the entrance hall above me. From the basement, I could hear his loud announcement. As usual, he wasn't talking *to* anyone other than himself. It was important that order be restored. I'd left the clock radio on the kitchen counter. It must be plugged in where it belonged, in the bedroom. The minivan must be parked in the garage.

David had been counting screws into bags or attaching color-coded plastic pieces to the ends of electronic wires at Tualatin Valley Workshop. His lift bus dropped him off in front of our house and he came inside.

I'd pulled into the driveway a few minutes earlier, the faces of fellow students at the five-day writer's workshop I'd just attended burning in my mind. Lois, Scott, Diane—I could see them as clearly as if we still sat together around the long table at Oregon's Linfield College. I'd left the minivan parked in the driveway, dropped the clock radio on the kitchen counter, and gone downstairs to throw a load of clothes in the washer. David's bus had come early, before I had a chance to put things away.

I'd timed my homecoming to arrive before David's bus. At fifty-three, I'd only once before been away from my family this long—to attend the same conference the previous year. The biggest problem, both this year and last, had been who would help David shave and wait for his bus in the morning, be home by 3:15 for his return, and take him to his dance, movie, or other activity on Monday evening. We knew no one outside the family who could fill in. Our two younger children both worked during the day and had their own activities at night.

The chores had fallen to Phil. "It's tough when you're gone," he'd said. This didn't lighten my decision to break away from my daily routine to sharpen my writing skills. When I'd called on Tuesday evening to see how things were going, Phil sounded tired and irritated. David's bus was late that morning. Traffic was bad and Phil was late for work. The house, I knew, would be clean; the laundry done. But what good was that if the mood had soured? How would I find things when I got home?

I rushed upstairs, eager to see David. A tall, thin twenty-six-year-old with light brown hair, in blue jeans and a red polo shirt, he stood at the kitchen sink scrubbing his black plastic lunch box—a daily ritual. Metal latches, rusted from repeated washing, clinked against the hard plastic sides. He kept his head down, intent on restoring the box to its original glory.

"David, how are you?"

He turned his head a few degrees in my direction. "Plug in the radio in?" He glanced at me for a second. The clock radio was still on the counter a few feet from the sink.

"Sure, you can put it away."

He set his lunch box down, wiped his hands on the green towel, picked up the clock radio, and strode off with it, almost in one motion.

His arms and legs swung rapidly as he power-walked toward the bedroom Phil and I shared. I knew he would be placing the clock radio on the nightstand next to the bed in exactly the same spot it had been before I left, as if he had a tape measure in his head. The way he always placed my yellow notepad two inches from the backsplash and two inches from the edge of the cupboard before leaving for work each morning. He would be reaching behind the stand to plug in the radio. I imagined him thinking, *There, everything's where it belongs. Everything except the new Dodge Caravan truck Mom needs to pull into the garage.*

I'd missed David while I was away. Had he thought of me only as another object out of its place? Did he ever visualize people in his mind's eye, as I had on my drive home from the workshop? Why didn't he seem to care about others?

I've searched my mind for signs that things used to be different. In one memory I've referenced, David is three. He bounces a shiny hair spray can around on the bathroom counter next to me as I put on lipstick. He dances the can over to a nearby cabinet, opens the door, edges the can inside, and closes the door.

Thinking back, I puzzle over this scene. Was he walking a doll to its house or parking a car in a garage? Did he have an imagination at three he now lacks? Maybe he was merely returning the can to its proper place, as he restored the clock radio to my nightstand and ordered the Dodge minivan put into our garage. But he did make it dance! The mother in me says so.

Since David can't tell me how he sees himself and other people, I look for clues. He's kept a decoupage above his bed since he was nine or ten: a depiction of a young Native American woman on a burro, gazing down at a swaddled infant laced to a board. The burro is trying to keep its footing on the edge of a rocky cliff. The baby's face is hooded. Only its cheeks, mouth and chin are visible. Both the mother and child seem as wooden as the board they're painted upon. To me, the child is a painfully restricted image, but the mother shows love in her gaze.

This decoupage came to us from my grandmother, who died many years ago. I don't remember how David acquired it, but it has survived three moves and has always been in the same position on his wall, while posters of skiers and rock stars and a print of Jesus, the

Good Shepherd—gifts from family and friends—are relegated to his closet.

How does David see this picture? I'd like to think he sees love in the mother's face—that he feels love in my gaze. But he can't read other people's emotions. Maybe he simply needs to feel he's safe; swaddled. Since other people are unpredictable, he searches for ways to contain them. For many years, he called one set of grandparents "Scappoose" and the other set "Tigard," identifying them by location. In his thirties, when our family was driving home from a vacation in Sunriver, he noticed how many cars were on the road: "Lots of car people."

I've felt despair over David's lack of interaction with others, but I remember how often he comes to sit with me at the kitchen table or stand behind me as I write at the computer. He also loves to be with relatives and friends, though he says little to them. He may be stuck in the stage psychologists call "parallel play." He wants to be near others but can't fully interact.

David's feelings about people may be similar to those Sean Barron describes in a book, *There's a Boy in Here*, written with his mother, Judy Barron. Looking back on his childhood with autism, Barron says, "Every time I turned on a light I knew what would happen. . . . People bothered me. I didn't know what they were for or what they would do to me. They were not always the same and I had no security with them at all. Even a person who was always nice to me might be different sometimes. Things didn't fit together for me with people. Even when I saw them a lot, they were still in pieces, and I couldn't connect them to anything."[7]

When I returned home from Linfield in July 1997, I didn't expect David to say, "Hi, Mom, how's it goin'?" His inability to communicate and connect emotionally with others is a big part of who he is. But I couldn't stop thinking and writing about him. Like the face of the infant in the decoupage, his face was hidden to me. I gazed at him not so much to be certain he was safe as to see who he was.

10

A Tale of Two Brothers
Using Ritual to Deal with Change

While David ate breakfast, I slipped downstairs to wake Jon for school. I peeked inside David's room. The covers were drawn over the pillows, the way David always made his bed. Carefully arranged Disney books lined a low bookcase. A single nightstand held only a radio—no lamp, because David didn't want one. The only objects on the dresser were the high school graduate statue and yellow soccer shin guards that had been there for years. The only picture was of the Indian woman on a burro gazing down at her swaddled infant.

When I opened the door to the next bedroom, a whiff of pot hit my nostrils. Rock posters plastered the walls. A spray of jeans, t-shirts, undershorts, socks, and pennies littered the carpet and every available surface. Blue sheets on the bed were empty, no boy inside.

By the time Jon was twelve, we often didn't know where he was. On advice from a counselor, Phil and I locked the doors and windows at 10 p.m. whether Jon was home or not. Sometimes, he'd be home at ten but missing in the morning. Other times, he'd be gone at ten but sleeping in his bed in the morning. How did he get into the house?

Once, at 3 a.m., I heard the screech of an aluminum window in the bedroom below ours. Years later, Jon confirmed he tapped on the glass and David let him in. After Jon moved away from home, we still heard David's window open during the night, as if he were letting in a ghost.

One time, after Jon had been missing for several days, he rang the doorbell at 6 a.m. Relieved to see him, I opened the door. A few months later, after Jon had again been missing for several days, David said at about the same time in the morning, "The doorbell will ring." Very soon, the bell rang. I looked out the kitchen window and saw David walking from our front door to the garage. He'd re-enacted Jon's earlier homecoming, in his own way bringing his brother home.

His actions reminded me Temple Grandin wrote that she relied upon doors and windows to help her adjust to changes in her life. Each time she graduated from school or changed direction in her studies, she found a door and practiced going through it until she felt confident enough to proceed. She also used a sliding window as a symbol to help her cope with the isolation of autism, which felt like being trapped between two panes of glass.[8] Although David lacks Grandin's superior reasoning ability and coping mechanisms, he developed ways to deal with his brother's comings and goings.

When Jon moved away from home, David insisted again and again, "Jon will bring his drawers back." He wanted his brother's chest of drawers returned to the bedroom where it belonged. As much as I wanted to believe David missed his brother more than his furniture, I knew he did miss his chest of drawers. Such seeming disregard for others can cause a family member to stop trying to make contact—especially if he or she is a teenager. When David ignores me or pulls back when I pat his arm, I can rationalize, "He responds this way because he has autism." A sibling finds such actions harder to accept.

There was a short period when Jon was eight or nine when he seemed proud of his older brother. He took friends into David's room to show them David's Special Olympics medals. A good athlete himself, he admired his older brother's physical achievements. A newspaper picture of Jon at six showed him running alongside David, urging him on at a track meet at Jesuit High School. Later, Jon distanced himself from the family as a whole.

Even if David hadn't been born with autism, he and Jon might not have been close. David is seven years older and reserved, while Jon is fun-loving and gregarious. David needs each person and physical object in its proper place; Jon has no such compulsions. But the disorder creates a barrier apart from age or personality differences: It robs them of the relationship they might have had.

11

Echolalia in Green

The Diagnosis of Bipolar and Obsessive-Compulsive Disorders

I lit the writing candle my friend, Nadine, gave me and settled in at the round table in our kitchen alcove. Rain hammered the skylight. The twining leaves and drooping tendrils of our ivy wallpaper were subdued in the low, flickering light. For ten minutes, I wrote about a dream I'd had early that morning of a baby in a man's suit who spoke and acted like an adult.

David bolted upstairs from the basement. "Change your clothes—clean, dry clothes!" In his blue bathrobe, he repeated my reminder a half-hour earlier to wear pants and a shirt from his dresser, not dirty ones from the hamper or wet ones from the washing machine.

"You need to get dressed. It's almost time for your bus." He had forty-five minutes, but the time it took him to get ready for work had increased from an hour to an hour-and-a-half.

"Your bus is here!" David bounded downstairs to his bedroom—at least, that's where I hoped he was going.

Twenty minutes later, he stood below the skylight, his back to me, facing the green countertop and dark window. A thin twenty-five-year old, he wore jeans and a denim shirt for his job at his workshop, where he packaged screws and electronic wires—when he was calm enough to work.

"Hurry up, put the dishes away," he reminded himself. For years, unloading the dishwasher and taking out the garbage had been his morning chores, along with making sure all books, magazines, and newspapers were perfectly stacked and sofa pillows standing at attention. But for the past few months, he'd had trouble focusing on any of these tasks.

Taking a white dinner plate from the dishwasher, he opened the cupboard door to put the plate away but set it on the counter instead. "You don't need to go through the garbage," he told himself. He opened the door and went down the steps into the garage, where he'd been saving trash in a green plastic bag in the corner—things that weren't recyclable, like cottage cheese container lids and empty ice cream cartons.

Finally, he came back into the kitchen and washed his hands. "Keep your hands out of the garbage," he scolded. It was fifteen minutes before his bus would arrive, and he hadn't eaten his breakfast. He walked from the kitchen to the family room to the living room, talking loudly: "June, July, August, September. Change the calendar to December . . . Hush up, be quiet . . . I'll be good, I'll be quiet . . . No school, Memorial Day . . . Last day of school . . ."

Each morning, he repeated a long litany of words others had said to him, his own responses, and statements related to the calendar. "No school, Memorial Day" and "Last day of school" had to do with my notes on the calendar for substitute teaching.

Finally, David ate Cheerios and drank a glass of orange juice.

"It's time to get your jacket," I reminded him.

"Get your jacket, get your jacket!" He went to the closet in the hallway and came back wearing his navy slicker.

He opened the cupboard door and ran his fingers inside the white bowl on the top shelf. "No money-quarters?" *Money-quarters* and *money-dollars* were his designations for cash. He knew about pennies, nickels, and dimes but didn't bother with them. He needed quarters for the vending machine at work. I was grateful he'd snapped out of his repetitive talk.

By the time I returned with the quarters, his bus had driven up to the curb and David had taken his lunch box and gone outside. I ran and reached the bus as the door was closing.

Back inside the house, I sat down again at the table. We had to help David and do it quickly. We were losing him; he was losing himself. He wanted to stop his echolalia and other repetitions, but couldn't. If he was home, I could hear his loud talking from every area of the house. When he got off his bus in the afternoon, I could hear him before he hit the front door: "Stop talking . . . Go to your work station . . . Stay out of the bathroom." Once I heard him shout, "If you don't shut up, I'll break your arm!" Had a co-worker threatened him?

It hadn't always been this way. In his early years, David played with toys, alone or alongside other children, but not with them. He had autistic traits, such as hand flapping and echolalia. But he was soft-spoken and even-tempered—not anxious. Once a waitress who was taking our order asked him, "What song are you singing?" He wasn't really singing; he was repeating in a sing-song voice, "Rain, rain, water down the drain." He often repeated jingles and advertising slogans such as "Dow has scrubbing bubbles." But these repetitions didn't take over his life.

Temple Grandin speculates in her book, *Thinking in Pictures,* "Children who are echolalic—who repeat what they hear—may be at a midpoint on the sensory processing continuum. Enough recognizable speech gets through for them to be able to repeat the words." She maintains that by repeating words, they verify they've heard them correctly.[9]

Grandin's theory explains David's repetitions as a child, but as an adult, his echolalia has often signaled stress. He tries to order his life, but each repetition only takes him back to his original position. It's as if he catches his foot in the same spoke of a bike wheel over and over again. It would be easy to dismiss his cyclical thoughts as the work of a dysfunctional brain, but I think how often I lie awake at night, turning over the same problem. Don't my thoughts sometimes get stuck, too?

David's first two years at the workshop after graduating from high school at twenty-one went smoothly. But the manager changed and the workshop lost contracts. The staff was supposed to do training during down-time, but they often held optional meetings about workers' rights and responsibilities— matters that meant nothing to David. Real work, make-work—they were the same to him. He needed consistency.

With time on his hands, David roamed the building, talking to himself. Recently, he'd begun a dangerous new practice: going outside. We received an incident report, "We found David hanging from the awning outside the building." The idea of a 6'3" man hanging from a window awning was humorous. But the next message was terrifying: "David crossed Alexander Street to throw paper over a fence. Nearly hit by a car."

On the recommendation of his case manager, Phil and I agreed David would see Dr. Ed Green, a psychiatrist in Portland who treated people with developmental disabilities. We set an appointment for early January. But as I sat at the kitchen table in early December 1996, I feared David would become stuck in one of his chants, divorced from reality. I would visit his workshop in Aloha again to search for clues to his worsening condition.

At the workshop, I walked over to a long table with a crooked mountain range of screws down the center. I knew some of the workers counting them into plastic bags from Special Olympics and Park and Recreation day trips. David was not at the table.

I found Frank, the supervisor. "Isn't this where David is working?" There were other tables in the large warehouse, with workers performing other jobs, such as shrink-wrapping and collating.

"Yeah, he's probably in the bathroom, cleaning." I knew what Frank meant. David was wiping the plumbing pipes down with pieces of toilet tissue. He often told himself, "Don't clean the drain pipes."

Frank went back to supervising. It was easier for him if David went on cleaning.

A woman with thick glasses and dark, curly hair came up to me. "Your son drives me nuts. He talks all the time." I recognized Denise, who rode David's bus. I was sure he did drive her nuts.

After waiting twenty minutes for David to return, I left.

It had been a frustrating few months. We'd appealed to an autism specialist, Randy Fulgham, to visit David's workshop and make recommendations for the staff. He'd gone even further, riding David's bus to work from our house and visiting us to see how we interacted with David.

One of Randy's observations was that David's work station and schedule frequently changed. He suggested the staff use a concrete calendar to help him cope with these changes. The calendar consisted of a four-part picture sequence. The first picture showed

David hanging up his coat and putting away his lunch; the second, his morning work task; the third, his break time; and the fourth, his afternoon work task. He was to turn each picture over after he completed the activity. But eventually Randy determined the staff didn't use the new system. Changing old habits was hard for them, as well as for David.

As David's anxiety increased, his fast walking and echolalia escalated. The more he talked, the more people around him asked him to be quiet. Their words echoed in his head, making him more anxious. Randy suggested the work staff and our family use hand signals instead of verbal instructions to eliminate the trigger for David's echolalia. Again, we failed. Either the practice required a consistency we couldn't maintain or it was impossible for David to accept the new system.

When Christmas arrived, David was still distraught. He tore the green wreath from the front door and replaced it with a bare grapevine wreath from a closet in the basement. He refused to open his presents. He didn't stay at the table long enough to eat his ham, cheesy potatoes and Waldorf salad. While the rest of the family worked on spumoni ice cream and chocolate crinkles, he stomped up and down stairs. "I'll be quiet. I won't be up, down, back and forth anymore!"

For the next three days, he tried to reinvent his favorite holiday, to reinvent himself: "I'm being good; I'm not repeating nonsense . . . I won't go up, down, back and forth anymore . . . I'll have a good tree with ornaments and lights."

As I sat in my robe and slippers in the living room on Sunday evening, trying to read the newspaper, he finally stopped his pacing and talking long enough to stand in front of my chair.

"Don't worry about Christmas Day?" I imagined he meant, "Am I all right? Is the world all right even though I missed Christmas? Should I forget how disappointed I am? Should I forget I didn't behave the way I wanted to?"

"It's okay. Just try to think about it in your head." I talked to him as if he were a young child—not a tall young man with autism—but I couldn't think of any other approach that might work, and I was tired of his repetitions.

"I'm sorry to make a memory in my head." He cupped his right hand over the left side of my head above my ear, as if to locate the place where memories originate.

I looked at him, amazed. His desire to understand had apparently overcome his aversion to touching someone. It was probably easier for him to imagine where the mind was located if he touched my head instead of his own. He needed a gesture he could see.

At twenty-five, he'd never spoken to me before about his mind or used the word *memory*. I felt sad that, when he took this important step, he thought he needed to apologize for what his mind had done. It wasn't the memories, but his loud talking, that got him into trouble.

A few weeks later, David poured Cheerios into the white bowl on the kitchen counter, filled the bowl with milk, and added two heaping spoonsful of sugar. "Had a bad dream." As usual, he spoke in a flat tone.

I stopped looking at the newspaper. He almost never talked about his experiences, let alone his dreams."

"What happened in your dream?"

"People say 'be quiet.'"

"Would they hurt you if you weren't quiet?"

He carried his cereal bowl to the table, sat down, and began to eat, his sharing finished.

David had been hearing "Be quiet, be quiet" at work and on his bus for several years now. And, as much as I hated to admit it, Phil, Lisa, and I said it, too. We asked him to be quiet when his talking drew attention at the grocery store, when it interfered with the stillness of a church service, and when we simply wanted quiet at home. Usually he complied with our requests. But sometimes his voice became louder, as if he insisted on being heard. Now, I wondered, shouldn't we try to hear his voice more clearly, rather than try to silence him?

Though David had a limited ability to understand what others were thinking, he'd picked up on their growing impatience. A few days earlier I'd heard him say to himself, "I'll be quiet. I'll be quiet forever." This had scared me. Did he think we wanted to silence him for good? Was it fair to ask him to be quiet when he couldn't stop talking and couldn't gage the volume of his voice? I wished he could assert his own rights. Since he couldn't express them, it was easy for others to ignore them.

I'd once seen these words of Eleanor Roosevelt's in a high school social studies classroom: "Where, after all, do human rights begin? In small places, close to home—so close and so small that they cannot be seen on any map of the world . . ."[10] But how were David's rights to be balanced with the rights of others?

The next month, we went to David's first appointment with his new psychiatrist, Dr. Ed Green. It was a getting-acquainted visit. As we were about to leave, Dr. Green said to David, "Will you come back and see me on St. Patrick's Day? Be sure to wear green!"

"I'll wear Dr. Green's clothes," David said as we drove away.

When David and I returned to Dr. Green's office in March, we both forgot to wear green. The doctor diagnosed rapid cycling bi-polar and obsessive-compulsive disorders and prescribed Clonidine and Depakote to alleviate the anxiety and short attention span. In a few months, he added Lithium.

For the next few years, David was prescribed a series of different medications, some more successful than others. But overall, the medications allowed him to focus and feel more comfortable with himself. His anxiety also decreased when we helped him move to a different workshop, Edwards Enterprises. Yet, loud, repetitive talking still sometimes made it hard for him to get along with others.

By his late twenties, his long monologues were mostly in the past. Though I was relieved he was calmer, I regretted the use of Lithium and tranquilizers to achieve this because they had serious side effects. I worried David always said "I'm fine" no matter how he felt. Strangely, I almost missed his monologues, because they gave us insight into his private world.

I think, for David, self-talk functioned as a sluice gate. As internal voices became too strong, he tried to expel them. But the more words he removed, the more remained. He wanted to be in control of his thoughts and feelings, but he wasn't. When he said, "I'm not repeating nonsense," he was right. His talk was repetitive and annoying, but it was not nonsense.

12

You Make Your Own Ham-Cheese-Pickle Sandwich
A Language Spurt

In spite of increased anxiety in his mid- to late-twenties, David's language became clearer and more colorful, even playful. "Be careful of that razor. Take your time, razor," he said as I helped him shave. "That's the real stinker-pits," he sympathized when I cut my finger rinsing a ragged soup can. "Need to find two pairs of ski socks . . . not short-sleeved, *long-sleeved* ski socks," he reminded me as I helped him pack for his Special Olympics Winter Games.

Many of these new expressions contained hyphenated words. Heavy rain wasn't simply rain; it was "pouring-down-weather-rain." Aspen Lake in Sunriver, long and skinny, was a "river-lake." A moth was a "moth-fly."

David also added new words to his vocabulary. "You need to keep on being quiet forever. You don't want to spoil people's fun," he admonished himself, using the words "forever" and "spoil" for the first time and showing that he realized his loud talking might bother others. As we watched a brutal battle scene in *The Lord of the Rings: The Two Towers*, he commented, "That's miserable," using a new and appropriate adjective.

He had never been able to describe his physical problems before. Now he made a start. His nasal drip in the spring was "clear blood." When he got athlete's foot, he reported pimples on his toes.

Not all of David's language attempts worked perfectly. Sometimes his grammar resembled that of a person from another country trying to learn English. One day, before going to the barber, he said, "Al's going to cut my hair rightly. He'll cut it shortly."

But as David's language became more precise, he was better able to express his wishes. When we stayed in our new vacation house in Sunriver for the first time, he and I inspected the loft where he'd sleep. I opened the sofa to show him the bed inside. "Don't want a bed-couch. Want a bed-ladder," he said in an even tone, registering disappointment he wouldn't have a bunk bed as he had in our previous vacation house.

An experience when David was twenty-eight showed how much his awareness of his surroundings and ability to talk about them had increased. David and I were driving to pick up Peter, a young man Phil and I paid to walk with David and take him to lunch or out for a coke or ice cream once a week. I'd told David we'd be picking Peter up at the transit center instead of meeting him at Commonwealth Lake, but David apparently hadn't caught my meaning. As we pulled into the left-turn lane to head from Cedar Hills Boulevard onto Barnes Road, he asked, "Are we going a different way?" I couldn't wait to write down his words! He'd used the right verb, the right pronoun, the right word order and the right inflection for a question. If he'd asked the question at all in previous years, he would have said, "We're going a different way?"

In addition to his other language gains, David began for the first time in his late twenties to address me as "Mom" and to ask questions beginning with "who," "what" and "where." He never asked "when" or "why" questions. (He did begin to use "when" in his thirties, as I describe in Chapter 13. In a few years he also protested, "Why, why, why?" if we couldn't take him on an outing, but he didn't listen for an answer.)

Looking back on David's communication breakthrough in his late twenties, it seems his early training and education laid the groundwork, but some skills needed to be solidified later. Another factor may be that David began taking medication for anxiety and bipolar disorder at twenty-six. He'd spent much of the previous year pacing and repeating others' words. Striding from room to room, he'd told himself, "Don't have time to walk around. Quit the walking around. I don't like the walking around."

Mostly free of echolalia in his late twenties, he was more able to focus on his own thoughts and the world around him. Yet, even before seeing a psychiatrist and taking psychotropic drugs to relieve anxiety, his language began to change. The best explanation for his language spurt seems to be that, like everyone, David learns on his own timetable.

One day in his late twenties, I realized how far he'd come since the dark days of his increased anxiety, echolalia, and other repetition. He was in the kitchen, making his lunch for work the next day, as I sat reading in the family room. Suddenly, I heard words very different from the self-incrimination I was used to hearing: "Look at that! You make your own ham-cheese-pickle sandwich. You're doing pretty good!"

And he was.

13

Pot Roast Coming Around the Clock
The Perception of Time

I watched from the family room as my tall, thin, twenty-eight-year-old son stood in the kitchen and followed a familiar ritual. His back to me, he wrote in the air with a blue pen an inch from the ivy wallpaper. On his left hung a wall calendar with a garden picture and my own scribbled notes: *10:30, Dr. Green; 12:30, lunch with Susan; 7:00, Edwards Board meeting.* With its grid of white squares, wood frame, and surrounding ivy, this calendar resembled a trellis holding the pieces of my life. Standing next to it, David seemed sadly in its margins—and more than a little strange.

I slipped an entry into my journal about his baffling behavior. I hoped an accumulation of such notes would help me understand my son and his unique way of seeing the world. The threads were as mysterious as David's writing in the air. Most puzzling of all were the entries about time.

For years, David had been obsessed with wall calendars. He'd patted them, arranged their pages, pressed them against the wall, and written in the air next to them. The previous year, his obsession had become even more puzzling. He wouldn't allow the calendar page at home to remain on April. "It's still March!" he insisted, flipping the page back each day. He refused to use his new April bus pass, declaring the March pass still good.

A supervisor at his workplace reported David was more obsessed than ever about the wall calendar in the hallway. After the old page had been ripped off each month, he frantically sifted through the trash, found the page, and taped it back. It seemed he could maintain a slight degree of control only if the calendar were whole.

Each month, David's psychiatrist tested David's anxiety level by flipping the calendar to the wrong month before our visit and watching his response. If David was very upset, he would spend minutes standing next to the calendar, fumbling with its pages, and moving the tack around on the wall. The calendar could only be on the wrong page if the month had just changed, and then it had to be on the previous month. As his anxiety lessened, he began to accept each new month a little sooner, allowing us to turn the calendar page to the correct month.

What caused David's calendar obsession? I thought back to his childhood and adolescence. Even more than most children, he'd loved repetition . . . predictability. At four, he'd pushed his rubber duck off the bathtub rim into the water again and again, each time crowing, "Poor dut." Like a baby playing peek-a-boo, he was learning events can create a pattern.

He'd insisted on leaving his empty Easter basket next to his bed all year, even as a teenager. Maybe he wanted to ensure Easter would return. He'd left his "little boy" shin guards on his dresser until he was twenty-five, perhaps hoping to play soccer again. When he was twelve, a coach had made him feel he could play the game. In reality, all he could do was kick the ball down the field and shoot it into the net. As he got older, there was no appropriate team for him, even in Special Olympics. But his hopes, attached to yellow shin guards, did not change.

David sat at the kitchen table, watching me as I washed onions. "Dinner will be soon?"

"Not for a while. Pot roast needs time to cook." I took out a cutting board and sliced an onion.

David was quiet for a moment. "Pot roast coming around the clock," he proclaimed suddenly, as though he'd figured something out.

I stopped chopping onions and looked at him, sitting under our schoolhouse clock. He seemed to envision pot roast riding on our clock's hands instead of simmering in the oven.

But, of course, this is how his life goes, I thought—food and services delivered to him. Much of his life is spent waiting—waiting for the lift bus to take him to work or bring him home, waiting for park district day trips to the beach or Mt. Hood, waiting for dinner. Waiting slows time.

But the image of the clock as a deliverer of objects may also explain why, as a child, he thought he could repair a music tape he'd hopelessly tangled or make wilted daisies raise their heads again. "They'll drink the water; they'll be okay," he said. Maybe it also explains why he left his Easter basket by his bed and his shin guards on his dresser, why he thought, even as a high school student, he would someday attend grade school again. If objects are pinned like donkey tails to a clock's hands, surely they will come around again.

The flow of time can be confusing even to those who do not have autism. The clock suggests a cyclical movement, as reflected in David's image of the pot roast circling it. But the calendar shows linear movement, even though days, weeks, months, and seasons repeat. Time even seems to have a vertical movement, suggested by expressions such as "sand through an hourglass" and "Let's get down to business."

The calendar also promises a stillness and control it doesn't deliver. Its boxes, lined up like soldiers, suggest that days, weeks, and months are separate— even equal. Yet, we know that past, present, and future flow together. Time doesn't march steadily forward. Instead, it lurches and languishes; staggers and falls back. It's not a soldier, but a mercurial phantom.

To cope with these contradictions, we use symbols and ceremonies. We mark the beginning of summer with a barbecue; the end of our workday with a happy hour or tea time. We celebrate a birthday or wedding with a cake, a memorial service with flowers. Symbols give our lives meaning and help us to go on. We learn to root ourselves in time.

Being rooted in time is difficult for someone who has autism, but easier when time is tied to objects and when events have a perceivable pattern. I wish I'd realized when David was younger how much he needs objects and ritual to help him navigate time. When he was five, he cried, "No, no!" each time I removed an ornament from the Christmas tree. Frantically, he tried to return it to its branch. I began to remove holiday decorations when he was not around.

In his early thirties, he said in a sing-song voice a few days after Christmas, "Gingerbread house teapot, put away. Christmas is all finished." He carried our red, white and green ceramic teapot from the kitchen to the cupboard in the hallway where we stored Christmas decorations. Maybe he'd needed an object to mark the end of the season.

When David patted the calendar, pressed it against the wall, fingered its pages, and wrote in the air next to it, he may have been showing his need for a tangible symbol of time. To some extent, this need is universal. When we remodeled our kitchen a few years ago, I felt disoriented when both the clock and calendar were removed. Though I was able to function, I was relieved when they were finally put back on our repapered walls. Later, I tried to move the calendar to our office and the clock to a different wall, but David moved them back to their original positions. His need for sameness is simply greater than mine.

As an adult, David's language has often showed his confusion about time. "I'll go to work today-tomorrow," he once said, showing he wasn't sure when one day became the next. Describing his work week, he said, "On Friday, you get down to home." Even now, he never says an event will happen next month, or next year. When I talk to him about an upcoming activity, I try to remember to say the day of the month and point to the calendar.

In spite of his confusion, David has made progress in talking about time. At thirty-three, he joined Phil and me for a vacation in Sunriver. I rewound the movie we'd just watched and put it back in its plastic case. "Will we take the movie tapes back to the store?" David asked. Then, pressing for more information, he said, *"When* will we take them back?" His voice, though still somewhat flat like Dustin Hoffman's in *Rain Man,* lifted slightly at the end. For the first time, he'd used the word "when."

I reached for my handbag. "We'll go now," I said to show him words have power.

What did David's writing in the air next to the calendar mean? In the beginning, I romanticized his ritual, seeing it as a yearning for a fuller life. If only he could push aside the ivy of our wallpaper, its pattern as repetitive as his own thoughts and behaviors, and slip into a "normal" life with his own friends and activities.

I had my life, with the usual freedoms; why couldn't he have his? I imagined him writing the things he would like to do if he could. The vapor trail of his words made me even more aware of what he was missing.

In truth, though, the words he wrote in the air were probably repetitions of what I'd written on the calendar or the calendar's notes about certain days—a kind of visual echolalia. He'd often copied a teacher or assistant's handwriting to learn to form words and sentences, and he liked to copy my words. He often incorporated calendar notations—"Mother's Day, Memorial Day, last day of school"—into his monologues, too.

David derives time's meaning from objects such as pot roast and the gingerbread house teapot, and from familiar patterns—as I do. Without his ritual of writing in the air, I would not have pictured the calendar as a trellis that provides structure and support. Without his announcement of pot roast circling the clock, I would not have understood as clearly the circularity of events and the importance of objects and patterns in our lives. We all need signs to mark our path through time. Those with autism simply need them more.

14

We'll Stop the Wind
Wishful Thinking

Columbia Gorge winds whistled over our house in northwest Portland. Ice built an igloo around us. Across the kitchen skylight, Hinoki cypress branches dragged relentless claws. David's bus dispatcher called to say the driver couldn't make it up our hill. We couldn't walk; we couldn't drive. Our newspaper and mail hadn't been delivered. Schools were closed. No one went anywhere unless they had to.

I sat beside David in the family room. I wished I'd poured hot water into a thermos before the power went out so we could have warm drinks. At least we had the gas fireplace. I remembered going outside with our daughter, Lisa, to get firewood by the garage the first year we'd moved to this neighborhood. There'd been an icy east wind like this one, and we could barely stand on the steep slope. We'd covered our faces with wool scarves and yet felt frozen in the time it took to get an armload of wood.

Our tabby groomed nervously by my feet as I sat on the hearth reading. A momentary hush was interrupted by the snap of alder branches in the woods. The rafters groaned with a huge gust of wind. Iced maple branches scraped the roof. I wanted to check the mailbox to see if the mail had come, but that would risk broken bones.

David said, "We'll stop the wind." His neck swung side to side—a slow pendulum of despair? "The trees won't fall down, they won't." Sleepy from his medication, he put his head down on the blue leather couch. Wind chimes clanged on the deck. Cold air seeped in around the single-pane aluminum patio door.

"You need a blanket." I moved to cover him with the afghan from the back of the sofa.

"I'll be fine." This was David's standard response when anyone offered a blanket or jacket. I couldn't stop myself from trying to make him more comfortable, though I knew what his answer would be.

David insisted the trees wouldn't fall, but two huge, split-trunked maples had plummeted the day before. With each loud thud, I'd rushed to the window to check the damage. The first tree to go down was the one in front of our living room windows, where we used to watch baby raccoons play in the branches. It fell toward the woods in back of our house. I would miss the raccoon family; the tree's shade in the summer and brilliant yellow leaves like lanterns in the fall.

The second tree to succumb was still caught in the branches of two slender firs next to our neighbor's backyard. If it went all the way down, it would ruin the new trees and shrubs they'd planted after a storm two years before. Our neighbor, Mary Ann, called minutes after the crash. "That tree went down just after I looked at it," she laughed. "I won't look out again!"

David raised his head from the couch. "The trees won't fall down, they won't."

I wasn't sure if he was talking about trees in the future or the past, since he often denied what had happened. "Do you mean the trees that already fell?"

"Yes." He squirmed.

Did he really think we could go back and redo what had happened, or did he merely wish it were so? When he was younger, he'd rescued the wilted daisies I'd thrown away, saying, "They'll drink the water. They'll be okay." Maybe he wanted to rescue the trees the same way.

As I sat by the fire, I felt protected, yet vulnerable. We can't stand to watch nature destroyed. The violence threatens our existence, too. As a friend said to me after the trees came down, "The shattering world shatters us."

During the storm, our family's world became smaller, more closed in. It seemed life was going on somewhere else without us. But was this any different from the way our life had been the past three years? Others have written about how people with autism are walled off from the world, with little interest in anything outside themselves. Their walled-in-ness can rub off on the family, too. At twenty-seven, David's anxiety and obsessive-compulsive disorder had not gotten much better. We'd tried to help him with monthly visits to his psychiatrist, but he was stuck in repetitive cycles, and we were stuck in these cycles with him.

In addition to David's vexing conditions, other family problems piled up like ice: Jon often stayed out all night, getting into trouble. A gnawing depression kept Lisa home, away from friends and the classes where she excelled. Phil felt anguish over his job and the children. I hadn't gone back to full-time teaching because the family needed me, but I worried I wasn't using my professional skills.

I had my own wishful thinking: David had finished college and was living on his own. Jon was finishing high school and on the track team. Lisa was a high school junior, playing flute in the band. Phil was doing the architectural drafting he loved, and I was teaching high school English.

Three days after David and I huddled by the fire, I stood in the living room looking into empty sky behind our house. The power was on, the wind had stopped, and the ice was melting. One tree lay across our backyard; the other still rested in the small firs next to our neighbor's property. A pickup pulled onto the concrete pad where our children played basketball. Two men got out and unloaded chainsaws.

David ran to the window to stand next to me. "Don't worry. They won't cut the trees. They won't!"

15

The Picture Frame Shop
Literal Thinking

When he was close to thirty, David rode in the back seat, behind me, as Phil drove us home from a week's vacation in Sunriver. Three snow-capped peaks loomed to our south. "The Three Sisters," I intoned and turned to see if David noticed the mountains. He stared straight ahead in silence. Why did I keep calling his attention to scenes? If I pointed out a bird or a ship or a waterfall, he wouldn't look at it.

Minutes passed before David asked, "They're in their house?"

Who was he talking about? . . . Oh, the sisters. So he *had* been paying attention but hadn't linked the name to mountains.

I tried again. "See those three mountains, David? They're called sisters because they're close together, like sisters." He looked as though he hadn't heard me. I might as well save my breath, I thought.

A half-hour later, we drove through the town of Sisters, with its stylish Western store fronts and hanging flower baskets. David looked out the window and chanted defiantly, "Sister's house, Sister's house." I realized then why he'd stared ahead when I talked about the snow-capped peaks. Not only did he have difficulty making the connection between what I was saying and what he was seeing, but in his mind, mountains would never be sisters and a town called Sisters would be home to women who were related.

I remembered how often I'd misunderstood explanations as a young child because I took them literally. At four, I'd gone with my mother to visit a friend in Portland. "Wait in the car," she said. "They have chicken pox." Since we lived down the road from a chicken farm, I knew that chickens pecked, and "pox" sounded like "peck." For the next few years, when I heard someone had chicken pox, I imagined chickens pecking under their house.

A few months after our Sunriver trip, David lightly touched the cover of the book I was reading in the living room and asked, "Is that the Good Shepherd at Christmas time?" I looked at the cover closely. An eye, painted with childish white strokes, dripped like a tear from the tip of a white cane. It *did* resemble a glittering ornament. The cane, like a staff, could have belonged to one of the shepherds in the Christmas story, who David mistakenly called the Good Shepherd. His interpretation fit his experience. As in our exchange about the mountains and the town of Sisters, he interpreted the objects literally. He couldn't know the poems in the book were about a father's blindness.

Since the eye was on a red background and hung from what looked like a hook, it must be a Christmas ornament. The cane must be a shepherd's staff.

I remember only one other time David alluded to art. We'd finished our lunch of tuna sandwiches and tomato soup and were clearing the kitchen table when he said, "Like the picture frame shop." Maybe he was talking about the art gallery in Cannon Beach where we'd gone to get paintings framed the previous week. The gallery had frames, but calling it a frame shop seemed to miss the point.

I wiped crumbs and soup smears from the table. "What do you like about the picture frame shop?"

He put his dirty soup bowl in the dishwasher. "Oh, picture frames . . ." his flat voice trailed off. "You hang them on the wall. They're fruit." His description missed everything I'd ever known and felt about art.

But then I gazed at the two watercolors in traditional gold frames on our kitchen wall, one of red and yellow Bartlett pears, tinged with green, on a burgundy cloth; the other of purple grapes, blueberries, and golden cantaloupe spilling from a turquoise bowl.

Was he marveling that you hang a picture on the wall and it magically becomes its objects? No, this would be far beyond his ability to contemplate.

Was he confusing the frame with its contents? I didn't think so. More likely, he simply found art easier to talk about in terms of a concrete object like a frame or fruit.

Even though David seldom talks about art, he probably feels at home with our family's water colors, prints, and oils because they're representational. Phil and I lean toward the literal, too.

16

Squishy Twinkies
Humor Based on Mental Images

My friend, Lillian, said her first thought when she learned of her young daughter's cognitive disability was that the girl would never understand family jokes. What a strange loss, I thought. But much of our shared human experience depends upon a sense of humor. If it's missing or impaired, how can we support one another through life's large and small moments? I began to wonder if David had a sense of humor, given his limited ability to understand everyday conversations and to empathize with others. If he had one, what kind of sense of humor was it?

When David's younger brother, Jon, was three, an uncle gave him a toy called Socko the Clown. A plastic figure filled with air, it was weighted to rebound each time the child punched it. I worried about what this toy would teach our children, but I guessed, rightly, its novelty would soon wear off. For the short time it was popular, David, ten, giggled each time Jon pummeled Socko and he sprang back up. The slapstick action, repeated again and again, struck his funny bone.

As I mentioned earlier, an occupational therapist recommended when David was a toddler that we buy him toys that showed cause and effect. From these objects, he would learn his actions had results and the world operated in a predictable way. Later, I described how David pushed his rubber duck off the bath tub rim as a young child, crowing "Poor dut" each time the duck hit the water. In his early school years, he loved "Duck, duck, goose" and "Ring Around the Rosie"— games that were physical and followed a pattern. Each time someone got tagged or the class shouted, "Ashes, ashes, all fall down," he giggled.

David's delight in a natural order of events continued as he got older. In his late teens and early twenties, he found glee in his younger brother getting into trouble again and again for the same transgressions. Once, he stood outside the downstairs laundry room where I was folding clothes and asked, "Who smokes there?" I stepped into the hall. Cigarette smoke wafted from Jon's room. David chuckled, delighted at the thought of his younger brother getting in trouble for something he himself would never do. He might have missed a lot in our family transactions, but he knew the rules. He knew if you broke a rule, you got in trouble. Breaking a rule was so outrageous, it was laughable.

David saw humor in life's smaller lessons, too. In his middle twenties, he remembered two events from his high school years. One day he told me, smiling mischievously, "Tim has squishy Twinkies. He put them in his backpack. Tim shouldn't do that." He seemed to have a mental image of Tim, who rode his bus for many years, finding the Twinkies and discovering his mistake. Soon after this, David told me a story about another school friend: "Heather sharpens her pencil too sharp. It gets too short." Again he smiled, as though seeing the pencil in his mind's eye. He seemed to feel satisfaction, knowing he would never put Twinkies in his backpack and sit on it, or sharpen his pencil too short. I was pleased he shared these memories because he usually couldn't express his thoughts.

In both instances, his humor was based on cause and effect and a strong mental image. If you put soft food in your backpack and sit against it, the food will get crushed; if you sharpen your pencil too much, it will become too short. Did he empathize with Tim and Heather? Probably not. He saw humor in what had happened to them, but I doubt he could identify with their frustration, any more than he could understand his brother's feelings.

A final example of how David sees humor in mental images and cause and effect came one morning during the ice storm that toppled our two maple trees. The wind had howled all night, and the power had gone out. I could stay home because the school district canceled classes, but Phil had to drive to his building specialties office to field phone calls from contractors who needed grab bars or toilet partitions. He took a flashlight into our dark bathroom to shave with his old safety razor.

"Oops, I shaved off an ear!" he joked as he walked back into the bedroom. From the hallway, David heard his father's quip and repeated the words loudly again and again, laughing hysterically as he power-walked to the kitchen. Phil and I laughed, too—one of our lighter moments.

David knew about safety razors and had been a little afraid of them. He'd never done a good job of shaving, so I did most of the job and let him finish it. Since he didn't like the noise and vibration of an electric shaver, we used a safety razor.

Though David can't share in all our family jokes, I take comfort in knowing he has a sense of humor—one that depends upon simple physical action, cause and effect, and clear mental images; one that can bring him pleasure and rub off on others.

17

I Don't Want to Go Outside
The Fear of Dogs

At twenty-nine, David could finally express his fear: "I don't want to go outside. I'm too afraid of the dogs." He was spending a weekend with Phil and me at our vacation house in Manzanita, a small beach town dubbed Muttszanita because it has so many dogs, especially during tourist season. They frolic in the surf and on the packed sand as their owners hurl a ball and watch them fetch. When I finally coaxed David to the beach, I steered him away from as many of the dreaded creatures as possible. Safely home, he reassured himself, "The dogs are nice and friendly." It seemed he wanted to believe this but couldn't.

Earlier that year, two people with dogs had approached us during a walk in Sunriver. David's body stiffened. "They won't hurt your face?" he asked, touching his cheek, as if he could feel their teeth biting into his flesh.

"No, they won't hurt you." I repeated the words I'd used since he was two.

He began walking but looked back from time to time to be sure the dogs weren't following him.

Phil traces David's fear of dogs to a time he took David for a walk when he was a toddler and a neighbor's dog jumped on him and knocked him down. I think he may be frightened by a dog's bark, since he has a heightened sense of hearing. He may be afraid of the animal's unpredictability, too. Whatever the reasons for his fear, our attempts to desensitize him to dogs haven't worked.

When David was eight, we moved to the house I mentioned earlier, where a neighbor's dog barked behind the fence near our kitchen and family room. The move itself was traumatic for David, who needs sameness in his life, but the disembodied barking delayed his adjustment to the move. He woke up at night, crying and talking about dogs as though he'd been dreaming about them. I found his tooth marks on the backs of our painted wooden dining chairs, the fireplace mantel, and the headboard of his bed. It seemed he was turning into his nemesis. Our pediatrician ordered tests for lead poisoning, and we were relieved when the results came back negative.

When David was sixteen, I took him trick-or-treating for the last time—partly because he had grown to adult size and partly because I could not control his encounters with dogs. As we walked through our neighborhood in the cold darkness, a dog suddenly started to bark in a side-yard. To escape, David climbed on top of a car parked in front of the house.

Afraid he would dent the roof or scrape the paint or the owner would have him arrested, I begged him, "Get down." He finally slid off the car's roof and raced down the street, stopping every few seconds to peer behind him.

When I caught up with him, I took his arm: "You can't trick or treat anymore." If he understood the reason, he didn't show it. At home, he put away his candy in the kitchen and tucked his batman costume and plastic pumpkin with a hole for treats on the top shelf in his closet, where they stayed for several years.

David's fear of dogs became a safety issue on almost every outing. Once, our family of five walked on a sidewalk next to the highway above the harbor at Depoe Bay. As the rest of us looked down at fishing boats, David saw a dog on the sidewalk ahead of us and darted into the street to avoid it. If the approaching car had been closer, the driver might not have been able to stop.

I ramped up my warnings to volunteers on David's Park and Recreation and Special Olympics trips with instructions to be especially vigilant if they were near a dog in a parking lot or by a street. We planned our walks to minimize encounters with dogs. At the coast, we took David to a neighboring beach with fewer dogs, so he could feel safe.

David's fear of dogs extended to other furry creatures, too. As a teenager, he barely tolerated our family cat and refused to go into the petting zoo with his younger brother and sister. Finally, he observed,

"Lions and tigers can't hurt you at the zoo." Because of his new awareness that the animals were caged, he felt safe.

He began to notice whether or not a dog was on a leash. If it wasn't on leash, his fear was as great as ever. Even now that David is older, we skirt the areas where dogs are off-leash or avoid the areas altogether.

18

The Real Thing
Hugs and Pronouns

My book bag lay on our round kitchen table, my jacket over a chair back. I'd spent my day cajoling chatty high school seniors a month from graduation who thought they could slack off for a substitute teacher.

On the green-tiled island, an icy, unopened can of Diet Coke sweated beads of moisture. Just what I needed. I picked up the cold can and headed into our office to check email. But before I could sit down at the computer, David strode into the room, snatched the can from my hand, and walked out the door.

"Hey, David," I yelled, "what are you doing?"

He returned and stood in the doorway, expressionless, without the pop. "Sorry to take the Coke. Next time I'll ask." It sounded like he was apologizing, but I didn't think so. In David's lexicon, *I* often means *you.*

I looked up at him. "Who needs to ask before taking the Coke?"

"Mom does."

So that was it: *I* was the soda thief.

Sometimes one has to be resourceful to get at David's meaning. Because of his autism, he doesn't process information the way most of us do. I've learned to ask questions if I don't understand his intentions.

I'd done something worse than snag a can of pop, though; I'd trespassed on David's turf. In some ways, food and drink define David in the way fancy clothes or cars or trips to Europe define others. His first "words" at two years of age were *dub-e-dub-e-dub* for potato chip and *ort* for orange juice. Now, at twenty-eight, food and drink were the only areas where he had some control.

David returned to the office and set the Coke can on my desk. I reached for it. It was almost empty. I gave him a frustrated grin.

His next action caught me off guard. Standing next to my chair, he placed one big hand on my chest and one on my back and squeezed, as if he had me in a vice. His hug, if that's what it was, was so mechanical I laughed.

"I love ya," he said, his voice flat like Rain Man's.

I couldn't remember the last time David had said "I love you," to me or anyone else. Sometimes, when he did say the words, I thought they were ones he wanted me to speak to him: "I, Mom, love you, David." They were a bid for attention, as when a woman says to her husband, "I love you," trying to get him to say the words back to her.

This time, it didn't really matter how David intended the words. His stiff-armed squeeze was a poor imitation of a hug, and I wasn't sure how he meant it, but I would consider it a hug. He'd taken my Coke, but he'd given me the real thing.

19

Bills and Tacos
Family Strife

"I hate living in this house!" Phil shouted from our office. Surprised by his outburst, I set my toothbrush and glass next to the sink in our bedroom and hurried across the hall. Phil stood in our office, frowning as he riffled through a pile of papers on his oak wrap-around desk. He looked as though he actually might leave the family and go to a sunny island in the Pacific.

"What's wrong?"

"I can't find the damn bills I paid last night. I put them on the kitchen counter. They were ready to put in the mailbox. Now they're gone." His gaze was fixed on the mountains of paperwork on his desk, the furrow between his brows deeper than ever.

"David probably put them back on your desk. Let me look." I began sorting through cascading envelopes on stacked trays and the adjacent piles of papers. David liked to pigeon-hole items where he thought they belonged. "He wouldn't have thrown them away," I insisted. David's actions were compulsive, but purposeful. The challenge was to understand his way of thinking. If we could learn his strategy, our daily life would be smoother, and we would function better as a family. Perhaps more important, we would see David as a person acting upon reasonable impulses, trying to create order in a disorganized world.

Yet, we couldn't find "the damn bills." In spite of my contention that David wouldn't have thrown them away, I went to check the garbage can under the kitchen sink and the can in the garage. Finding nothing that resembled newly addressed envelopes, I returned to the office.

Lisa, our nineteen-year-old daughter, joined the search. "The bills must be on the desk. It's where David would put them," she said, as she thumbed through the old bank statements and envelopes of receipts lined up diagonally from the front center of the desk to the back corner. "Aha!" She plucked out a parcel of clean, stamped envelopes and held them up to her dad.

How had we missed them? David had tucked the out-going mail in with the long-ago incoming mail, as he tucked dirty shirts between clean ones—never on top, always in the middle, as though hiding them. The bills were in a logical place, though. And he *had* cleared the kitchen counter before he went to work.

Still frowning, Phil took the bills and left.

Since his teenage years, David has had trouble leaving other people's paperwork alone. He'd tell himself, "Don't go in the office," but the temptation was too great. He plastered stamps on blank sheets, tore church offering envelopes from their book, and reorganized tax information. We considered putting a lock on the office, but since both Phil's desk and mine were in the room, we would have been constantly locking and unlocking the door. I wonder now, why didn't we try giving David his own "offering licking envelopes" (envelopes with a flap to lick) and his own desk?

The more Phil and David tried to exert their respective wills against the out-of-control paperwork, the worse the problem became. I offered to handle the bill paying, or at least share the responsibilities, but Phil said he had to juggle finances to get everything paid. Relieved, I let him juggle them. Looking back now, I understand the pressure he was under and wish I'd done more to help him.

The last few years had been hard for Phil. He'd toughed it out through the death of his father, the news that his first child had been born with a disability, and the loss of his family business during an economic downturn in the eighties. He never missed a day of work or suggested he might leave the family because our troubles were too great to handle. He went every day to a job he disliked because he was afraid if he moved to a different job, he wouldn't earn enough to support our family. This was a legitimate concern since I earned very little as a substitute teacher. Now, even his attempt to pay the bills had been thwarted.

An incident a month later showed how deep the rift between Phil and David—and between Phil and me—had become. I'd made tacos for dinner. In what was now our usual practice, I called David to the table at 5:30 and served him dinner. Jon had moved into an apartment with friends and Lisa had an evening class. Phil sat in the family room with a drink, watching the evening news. I poured a glass of wine and joined him, leaving David to eat at the kitchen table alone.

"Nice tie, Peter," Phil said to the anchorman, who was cueing the White House correspondent. During a commercial break, Phil went into the kitchen to refill his glass. I heard him shout, "Don't eat any more tacos! Think about Mom and Lisa." He didn't say, "Think about Dad." I wished he didn't always put himself last.

When Phil returned to his place next to me on the loveseat, I turned to him. "You know, the Depakote makes David really hungry." I was referring to the mood-stabilizing medication Dr. Green had prescribed. "Kathy at church gained forty pounds on it."

Phil was quiet, watching the TV. More and more, I found myself making excuses for David, speaking on his behalf. I felt caught between his interests and Phil's and wasn't sure how to handle the tension. The week before, at a restaurant, the waiter had asked David, "Do you want a refill on your Coke?" David answered yes, but Phil said no. The waiter came back to ask, "Would you like dessert?" David said, "Have a cookie?" Phil said, "No."

"Do you want to talk about this later?" I asked.

"No, let's talk about it now."

"We can't treat David like a kid."

"Well, he acts like one."

"But he's not. We have to try to look at it from his point of view . . . and it would help if we ate dinner together."

As we talked, David came into the room and sat on the blue leather couch for a few moments, but didn't say anything. He got up and walked to the kitchen, then back to the couch, passing between the TV and loveseat each time. The friction of David's pants sliding over the edge of the cushion had worn the leather so that the piping on the edge and part of the cushion itself were no longer blue, but brown. The friction on Phil as David passed back and forth in front of us was just as apparent.

I went to make more tacos. Phil and I ate them in front of the TV. He went to bed and I sat reading a book of poetry I'd bought that day and drank another glass of wine.

In a few minutes, David came into the room. "The tacos were too gone?" He was using me as his sounding board.

"Yes."

He sat down on his worn cushion and frowned at me, as if trying to figure things out. "Dad doesn't like you?" he said finally. Since he almost always referred to himself as *you,* I knew he meant, "Dad doesn't like *me?"*

I hesitated a moment. I wanted to make things better between David and Phil, but I didn't know how. "Of course Dad likes you. He just wants you to think about other people." Thinking about others was a familiar topic. It seemed an impossible task for David.

He looked puzzled as he left the room. I was sad he thought his father might not like him. But later, I realized he'd reached an important milestone: He'd tried to imagine how someone else might feel.

The next morning, Phil left for his 6:00 exercise class and I lay in bed, dozing. Since I didn't have to work that day, I planned to jump out of bed at 6:45 to help David shave and be sure he had everything for work before his bus picked him up at 7:15.

I was asleep when David burst into the bedroom, talking loudly to himself about what pants to wear to work. "Wear the jeans, not the Sunday School pants," he said, as if he didn't make that choice every work day. He strode across the room to our mirrored closet doors.

"Don't wake me up. I don't like it!" I shouted, half-asleep, as impatient with David's habits as Phil had been. I'd begun to think of myself as a glider plane floating in the path of our family's situation.

David bent down next to Phil's closet and retrieved his box of shoes from the floor without saying anything. When the shoes were new, he'd donated them to his father so he could keep wearing his old, familiar shoes. He passed off new clothes and shoes to his brother the same way. He never asked if anyone wanted his things; he just put them in their closet. Recently, he'd started wearing the shoes he kept in our bedroom—maybe they were old enough now—but his storage place remained the same. Each evening, he put the shoes away in their box in Phil's closet; the next morning, he came to collect them.

I thought my earlier protest hadn't registered with David, but that night, as I worked at my desk, he walked by the office, repeating, "Don't woke me up, I don't like it!" He echoed the words I'd shouted that morning, but with a new awareness of verb tense, had changed the verb *wake* to *woke*.

When David charged into my bedroom that morning, he probably didn't realize he was bothering me, since he isn't able to put himself in another person's place. But my angry protest got through to him. His repetition of my words reminded me how powerful my parent voice is. It also made me realize that, like most people, David remembers admonitions more than praise. I needed to remind myself, no matter how challenging his behaviors, to show him love and respect.

Phyllis Mannan

IV.

When the news page lifted
from the small table and floated
to the ground next to our deck chairs,
David said, "Wind paper."

Phyllis Mannan

20

It Was Not Impossible
The Move to a Group Home

"You'll be better at the beach. You'll change your life," David said, as he drank the last drops of milk from his cereal bowl. It took me a minute or two to realize he was talking about the previous week at our beach house, when his pacing and loud talking had been worse than usual. It was like him to use advertising slogans such as "It's better at the beach" and "You need to change your life." It was also like him to mull over past behavior, vowing things would be better next time.

Later that week, I was in the kitchen thinking about dinner when the phone rang. It was Tom Foster, David's county case manager. After asking how things were going, he said, "By the way, David's name just came up on the wait list for residential services."

I held my breath for a moment before asking, "Are you sure that's right?" *This can't be,* I thought. *There must be some mistake.* The last we'd heard, David was over fortieth on the list.

"It's true," Tom insisted. "A group home in Tualatin has two openings. There's a live-in person, but no one on duty twenty-four hours. Residents have to be self-sufficient during the night . . . David is, isn't he?" I supposed he was; I really hadn't thought about it.

Not everyone on the list had qualified. Some were the wrong gender, some needed too much care, and others were not a good fit for various reasons. A few families had turned the spot down. We had to act quickly if we wanted David to be considered. The home couldn't operate long with only three residents.

I was quiet as Tom described the process we would follow if we were interested. Phil and I would visit first. If we thought the home might work, we'd take David to visit and meet the program manager. If that went all right, David would have a trial sleepover.

This must be a mistake, I thought again as I hung up. We'd put David's name on the wait list for both vocational and residential services when he turned sixteen. Now he was thirty. He'd received a vocational slot about eight years earlier, but residential services? Forget it. In Oregon, the wait list had become a joke among parents waiting for services for their adult children with developmental disabilities. There was no movement unless someone died, and then the spot was taken by a client in crisis, where the family could no longer provide care. We knew at least a dozen people with a child whose name had been on the list for residential services longer than David's. We'd talked to some of them about finding an old house and fixing it up, hiring staff, and running the home ourselves. But state regulations and staffing would have been horrendous.

When Phil got home from work, I told him about Tom's call before he even took off his jacket. "You won't believe what just happened." I told him the news.

"But Tualatin's too far." Next door would have been too far. Neither of us could imagine David living anywhere but with us.

I gave him a hug. "It's just down Highway 217 and a little ways on I-5—probably only twenty or twenty-five minutes."

Finally, we agreed we had to visit the home. This might be David's only chance at a life apart from us. We were in our late fifties. What if we died, or could no longer provide a home for him? Wasn't it better that he make the adjustment of moving while we could help him?

The next Thursday, Phil and I pulled up to an ordinary cream-colored house on a cul-de-sac in Tualatin, a suburb south of Portland. The paint on the garage was peeling and part of the driveway was raised where tree roots pushed up the asphalt . . . but graceful fir trees lined the back of the property. I reminded myself it was not the building, but the people, that mattered.

The home was operated by Good Shepherd Communities, formerly Good Shepherd Lutheran Home of the West. Part of a Lutheran family from birth, I'd gone with my mother to visit the large Good Shepherd campus in Cornelius when I was young. I remembered big, three-wheeled cycles outside the entrance and long halls leading to residents' rooms. In the push to create more family-like settings for residents in the 1990s, that facility closed. It was replaced by ten-person homes, and later five-person homes, in the community.

My experience with group homes was limited to a few years in which I'd given rides to a young woman who attended our church. The staff at her residence often changed and she moved twice in one year. Was this typical? I didn't want David to have to move after he'd settled in.

Paul, the live-in at the home, met us at the door and showed us around. There were four bedrooms and two baths. Paul used the larger back bedroom and adjoining bath. When there were five residents, four doubled up in two bedrooms, and the fifth had his own room. David had always had his own bedroom. Would he have to share one if he moved in? After all, he would be the newcomer.

Paul led us into the living room, looking over his shoulder. "The three guys who live here came out of Fairview when they first started putting people into homes."

Fairview Training Center had been Oregon's institution for people with developmental disabilities. It released residents into the community in waves. I hadn't shaken my fear of the place, which had closed the year before. Once called the Institution for the Feeble-minded, it was lumped in many people's minds with the Oregon State Mental Hospital. Both were investigated for years for alleged abuses. I'd once talked to a mother who'd sent her son to Fairview because he'd grown too big to handle. He'd thrown his food across the room, hit, and kicked her. She was grief-stricken by her decision to send him away, as she called it. We read news accounts of children who didn't know their own names, who sat on benches for hours, waiting to have their teeth brushed.

"This is Joe," Paul said. A gray-haired man about seventy sat in a rocker, riffling through a magazine. Smiling, he put the magazine over his head as if to hide. "Joe and Jack, over there, are both nonverbal." I hoped there would be someone for David to talk to, though he wasn't outgoing.

Soon a large, smiling, dark-haired man in a black felt hat and black vest walked up to me and extended his right hand. "I'm Wes." He led me by the hand into a small, u-shaped kitchen with dark cabinets. "Looky here. This is where we fix our food." I no longer worried that David wouldn't have anyone to talk to or that he wouldn't have anything to eat. Wes would befriend him.

Paul motioned us out of the kitchen and into the dining area, where the third resident, Jack, sat on a cracked vinyl chair at the table, coloring a picture of Snow White. We said hi. He glanced up briefly and went on coloring, careful to stay inside the lines.

A small TV, file cabinets, and a desk lined the walls. On the brick mantel hung a picture of Jesus with blue eyes and flowing brown hair. Tacked to the bulletin board was a memorial service folder with a photo of a man in a black beret. Wes explained this was his friend who recently died. The truth struck me: *Someone had to die in order for David to have this opportunity, this opening . . . this "slot."* The system seemed so impersonal.

Paul opened the glass patio door. "Jack likes to chop wood back here."

We stepped out onto the deck. Below a wooded hillside, a few pieces of firewood and a small shovel lay on the dirt bank. "We let Jack use that shovel to chop his wood. He's always doing something—mopping the floor, coloring pictures . . . We heard he lived with his grandmother on a farm before he went to Fairview."

As we drove home, Phil and I were silent. I'd always been afraid of "sending David away." I was glad he'd never lived at Fairview. But a group home was different from an institution, I told myself. It would offer him an opportunity to be part of a family and a community. Jack had choices he hadn't had in the institution. He and the other two residents were quiet. Paul seemed caring. The problem was David himself. Although he'd been quiet and even-tempered as a child, now his words and behaviors were often loud and repetitive. How would the staff and residents respond to him? And could he adjust to their routines? Unlike Jack, he didn't find ways to occupy himself. What would he do in a group home?

But I'd read even the dreaded Fairview had a place called the Possible Building. Much better than Fairview, 89th Court was a place of possibilities—a possible home.

Before David's first visit to the group home, I took him to Al's Barber Shop in Cedar Mill for a haircut. David walked ahead of me through the glass door.

"Hello, David." Al looked up from cutting a young boy's hair and greeted David with the same familiarity and respect he greeted everyone who entered his shop. He wore his usual dark polo shirt and a black band below his right elbow. Two other barbers, Bill and Paul, worked next to Al along the mirrored wall. On the floor surrounding their chairs was a thick duff of brown, black, red, yellow, and gray hair.

David didn't say hello to Al, but I did. During the fifteen years Al had been cutting David's hair, I'd come to think of him as a friend. Anyone who treats David well is a friend. I often stood by the door and talked to him while he cut David's hair, filling him in on family events and David's Special Olympics trips. My husband, brother-in-law, and nephew went to Al, too. He even attended our nephew's high school basketball games.

David paused at the candy machine near the door. "Need money-quarters." It would have been best if David could have handled his own money, but he seemed disinterested in doing this and had never learned to make change. I gave him a quarter. He stooped, put it into the slot, and held out his hand for a few bright M & M's.

I looked for a place to sit. There were a dozen men and a woman, apparently waiting for the small boy in Al's chair. They sat in webbed outdoor chairs. David took the only seat left, between two men craning to watch a baseball game on an old console TV in the corner.

"Over here, David." I took two wooden chairs from the back room and placed them in the doorway between the back area and main room. If I sat next to David, I could whisper, "Use your indoor voice" if he spoke too loudly and encourage him to wait his turn with the barber. As we sat in the doorway, I read a friend's poems.

"Cut that hair, barber," David said, laughing. Most of the time, though, he was quiet.

When Paul nodded to a man two chairs down from us to come forward for his haircut, the man said, "Waiting for Al." Another person went to the barber seat in his place. This process repeated a few minutes later when Bill had an opening. Paul and Bill never nodded at David; they knew he waited for Al.

The man next to me smiled. "Waiting for Al's a mistake, it seems." He had white hair, a white beard, and nice, even features. I smiled back. I didn't mind waiting as long as David was quiet. Al gave David the best haircut, and I wanted to tell him about David's chance for a group home.

After twenty minutes, Al nodded to the man next to me. He got up and walked stiffly to the barber chair. "Eyebrows, too," he told Al. "I can't see what I'm doing with these eyebrows." The clippers whined as Al attacked the man's white hair. David was quiet as I read my friend's poems.

The man looked out the window. "Does the Grange still meet there?" He pointed to a dilapidated building across the street.

Al glanced up. "I think so."

The man squinted through his long fringe of eyebrows, as if looking into the past. "My grandparents moved here to the valley in 1901. This used to be all farmland."

Al was finishing up, trimming the man's beard and eyebrows with a pair of scissors.

The Tualatin Valley had changed a lot in the past hundred years, but human kindness hadn't changed. Al's Barber Shop was a sanctuary from the busy outside world. I felt a pang of regret. If David moved to the group home, I might not get to wait for Al. My life would change, too.

On a cool evening in late April, we took David to visit 89th Court. Jennifer, the manager, met us at the door. A soft-spoken woman about David's age, she talked to him about Special Olympics cross-country skiing and basketball. In the next few days, whenever we talked about the group home, David called it "Jennifer's house." I saw his identification with

Jennifer as a boon. If he was accepted by the home, it would make his transition to living apart from us easier. But we had to get through the sleepover, and he was pacing and talking loudly, as he had at the beach.

After David got home from work on Friday, I helped him load his toiletries and an extra pair of clothes into a Nike duffel bag and we drove in rush hour traffic to Tualatin. I parked and David and I got out of the car.

When I rang the doorbell, a dark-skinned man opened the door. "I am Nyamu." I hadn't realized the weekend staff would be different from the staff on weekdays. Jennifer had won David over by talking to him about Special Olympics, but Jennifer wasn't here. How would he respond?

"He will be fine," Nyamu reassured me in the perfect grammar of one who has learned English as a second language. But when I returned the next morning, he reluctantly said David had paced and talked loudly most of the night. Nyamu could not have gotten much sleep. David's case manager was clear: This was not a twenty-four hour house. Residents must be able to take care of themselves during the night, so the live-in staff person could sleep.

I felt an enormous let-down. I'd convinced myself David's move to the group home would be good for him and our family. Now the move wouldn't happen.

I started to gather up David's things. "I'm so sorry. I don't think it will work for David to live here."

"It was not impossible," Nyamu said in his impeccable English.

I looked at him in amazement. He seemed willing to give David the benefit of the doubt and to put his own sleeplessness aside.

Jennifer called on Monday to say David could do a second sleep-over. The next time he stayed at the group home, he did much better, and the date of May 15th was set for his move. Nyamu's acceptance of David's difficulties provided an opening. If he hadn't spoken on David's behalf, there might not have been a second chance. This home—89th Court—was truly a place of possibilities.

In the next two weeks, I wondered how many of David's things we should take to the group home. He would need a few clothes and some bedding for the new long twin mattress, a duplication of the bed he had in his room at our house. I thought he would want his radio, his picture of the Native American woman and her baby on a burro, and his Disney books. What about the old soccer shin guards from when he was fifteen, the plastic statue of a Sunset High School graduate in purple cap and gown, the aftershave he never used, and the Disney postcard—items lined up on his dresser? What about the dresser itself? Would he remove these things from his old bedroom to take them to the new one? Old, new . . . one object or place becomes old as it's replaced by another. But David can never accept change. And would he understand this was not another visit, that he would be living at 89th Court?

We worked out a plan for the first week. David would spend Tuesday, Wednesday, and Thursday nights at the group home, going to work in Hillsboro on the bus each day. On Friday, he would come to our house after work (I hoped the driver would remember to bring him there instead of to the group home). On Saturday, Phil or I would take him to the Park and Recreation District bus for a canoeing day trip he'd looked forward to.

These were the logistics. The emotional dynamic was something else: Would the move work? Would David actually sleep at the group home? Would his loud talking increase because of anxiety, as it had during his first sleepover? Would he be able to adjust to so many changes at once—a new house, new location, new family, new bus driver, new food? This would be a lot for anyone to handle, let alone a person with autism. But, as Nyamu had said, it was not impossible.

On Mother's day, I took a picture of the three kids standing on our back deck—Jon and Lisa leaning close like brother and sister, David standing stiffly apart like an older uncle. I wanted to capture the children together before David's move two days later. It seemed after that, our family would never be the same again.

But when Tuesday came, the event seemed more like another trial sleepover than a move. I'd tried to involve David in packing the day before, but he wasn't interested. "Don't need to pack," he said. He didn't seem to understand what was happening. I felt we were betraying him. Had we made the wrong decision?

After I got home from work on Tuesday, I tucked his toiletries and a few clothes into his red Nike duffel bag, boxed his Disney books and the figurines Lisa had given him, his radio and some bedding for the new long twin mattress, and put them in the minivan. David's bus dropped him off, and Phil arrived. Finally, after David was sitting in the car waiting to leave, I took his decoupage of the Native American woman and her baby off the wall near his bed and grabbed his lunch box from the kitchen. We'd decided to leave his dresser and nightstand behind. David would want his room to look the same when he came back to our house on Friday.

When we got to 89th Court, the first thing I did was to show David where to put his lunch box. The staff agreed he could keep it on the kitchen counter, as he'd done at our house.

In the bedroom, Phil and I pushed David's new bed next to the window and made it as he watched. Phil hung the decoupage on the wall. "Is this okay, David?" I asked. He didn't answer or even look in my direction. I helped him line up his Disney books and figurines on a shelf next to the bed. Peter Pan and the wooden Indian mother would look after him.

I felt as though I'd lost part of myself when we left David sitting in the living room with his new housemates, though we'd see him in only three days. He didn't look at us, so I had no way of knowing how he felt. The case manager said the first month would be a trial period, but it seemed our lives had changed irreparably.

As the days and weeks went by, we were amazed how well David adjusted to his new life. Three months after the move, when he visited us for a weekend, he asked on Saturday afternoon, "Go back to the group home?"

"Jennifer doesn't expect you to come back until Sunday."

"Tell her we changed our mind," he said, handing me the phone—this from a person who never communicated by phone and had never before talked about anyone changing their mind! How had he learned this new expression?

For the next few months, David and I went back to Al for his haircuts. Gradually, the group home staff began taking him to a shop where the other men got their hair cut.

Six months after the move, I picked David up for lunch at Applebee's. It was Saturday, so the restaurant was crowded. We sank into a comfortable booth near the bar where we could see Tiger Woods on a big screen. Tiffany-style light fixtures, photos of Corvettes and Ferraris, and sports and movie memorabilia lit up the place.

In any restaurant, except a loud burger or pizza joint, I worried David's loud talking would bother the people around us. But when I asked what he was doing at work, he said softly, "Doing boxes." For years this had been his response, though his job involved putting items into bags, not boxes. His reply could have gone back to high school where he'd learned a variety of vocational tasks. I looked at him, sitting across from me, glad he hadn't changed. I couldn't believe how well he'd settled into his new life. His striped shirt and jeans were rumpled, but that didn't matter.

I was getting used to our new relationship. Before David moved to the group home, it had been easy to gage his needs. I'd seen him every day except for a handful of times he stayed with grandparents or went away for a Special Olympics competition. Now, I had to find occasions for us to be together so I could show him we cared and reassure myself he was still the son I knew—or tried to know.

Since David went to his workshop Monday through Friday, weekends were the best time to see him, but the group home, with four housemates and two staff, didn't provide the best venue. If David didn't come to our house on the weekend, Phil and I often took him to lunch. Today Phil was busy, so I'd come alone.

"Here, David, let's look at the menu." I handed him one.

He glanced at the glossy pictures of shrimp, steak, and burgers. "Shrimp," he said quickly. That was easy. But sometimes he'd change his mind after he ordered and the waiter or waitress walked away. Then I'd have to say, "I'm sorry, but we already ordered." He never insisted on his new selection, but I could see his regret: Something had been taken away from him and from our time together. I wanted to avoid that this time.

"Are you sure?"

"Yeah, sure."

"Garlic mashed potatoes or fries?"

"Garlic mashed potatoes." He pointed to the picture on the menu. Was he choosing them only because of the picture? But then I remembered he liked his grandmother's garlic potatoes.

The young, dark-haired waiter brought our drinks. I sipped my iced tea and looked at the menu. We could get two meals with beverages and an appetizer for twenty dollars. Oriental grilled chicken salad sounded good. But *Oriental*—wasn't that a disparaging term? I'd dealt with labels for developmental disability so long I was sensitive to all labels for people and cultures. I put my skepticism aside and ordered the salad anyway.

"What would you like, sir?" The waiter looked at David.

David mumbled his order. I chose spinach and artichoke dip as an appetizer, and the waiter left.

I leaned across the table. "Did you hear what he called you, David? He called you sir!"

David took a sip of root beer from his straw. Looking down at the glass, he said without expression, "Sir and lady."

After his words sank in, I basked in their significance. After so many years of feeling awkward as others stared at us in public places, I felt, at least for the moment, honored. According to David, we weren't merely equals but members of a royal class. Did he see himself as an adult now that he was living away from his parents? Had his move marked a change in our relationship? I wished he could tell me more.

My relationship with David has been different from my relationship with my other two children; he can't carry on a conversation with reciprocal thoughts or establish emotional rapport. But now he had done this, if briefly. He'd thought beyond himself and shown imagination. Not only had he understood that the waiter called him sir, but he'd extended the title to include me.

I thought about the young man who had given us the gift of calling him *sir*. When David was a child, a waitress at Shari's had told him he was special and given him an extra dessert. She meant well, but I wanted her to treat him like any other child. When he was a teenager and a young adult, his immature behavior prompted waitresses to call him *honey* and to look to us, his parents, to supply his order.

Now, when David was thirty, a waiter had looked him in the eye and called him *sir*. Had he passed for normal? His loud, unusual speech, blank or exaggerated facial expression, and lack of eye contact usually gave him away. I decided the young waiter had realized his disability and chosen to ignore it.

More and more, David was becoming his own person and we were getting used to seeing him as an individual apart from our family. His move to a group home was the right thing—for him, and for us.

21

I Like to Be a Clown
Resistance to Parental Control

I was slicing cucumbers and tomatoes for a salad when David peered down from the loft. "Do you like it here?" Although he seemed to be asking me this question, I knew he was really asking himself. He knew vacations should be fun, but he wanted to eat dinner every day at five o'clock, as he did at his group home. He wanted to decide how long to wear his underwear before it was washed. And he wanted to wear his shoes in the house.

This had been the first full day of a week-long vacation in Sunriver. That morning, Phil, David, and I had come into the house through the garage after our walk. I removed my tennis shoes and placed them at the bottom of the steps next to the furnace. Phil took off his Reeboks and put them next to mine. David started up the stairs.

"We leave our shoes here, David." I hoped he would comply without a struggle. He knew the rule. The pine residue on the paths turns the soles of our shoes black. After spot-cleaning the cream-colored carpet each time we visited, we'd agreed with relatives who also used the house to take off our shoes. I remembered David's new pair of cross-trainers at his home, still in their original box. Maybe we should have brought them. But the reason they were in the box was simple: David doesn't like to wear new things.

He bent over and slipped off his cracked, dirty, white shoes with frayed laces. Instead of leaving them by the furnace, he carried them up the steps into the house.

I imagined he was taking them to the loft he always chose instead of a bedroom. It has a hide-a-bed, three chairs, a trunk, and a TV, and gives him some distance from his parents. I think he also likes the novelty of looking down on us.

A few minutes later, as I put away laundry, I saw David walking in the hallway, wearing his shoes.

"Remember, we take our shoes off in the house." I was gritting my teeth.

"Take the shoes off!" David scrambled up the stairs to the loft. When he thinks a request is unfair—or he's being treated as a child—he repeats the instructions in a loud, angry voice. I tell myself he's limited in his choices; he tries to protect what freedom he has. And it's almost impossible for him to change his habits about even the smallest things.

It would not work to have him wear slippers in the house if he's always worn tennis shoes. When he was young, he willingly took off his shoes when he came in from playing outside. At thirty-six, was he going through an extended adolescence?

After lunch, I sat reading on the back deck. Through the patio screen, I heard Phil shout in the kitchen, "Don't use the sponge on the shoes, David . . . If I say don't, don't do it!" He must have caught David washing his shoes with the kitchen sponge.

"Don't use the sponge, don't do it!" David mimicked his father. I knew he would be racing from the kitchen into the living room and down the hallway, his anxiety escalating.

We'd been on vacation two days, but it felt like two weeks. I'd thought we would have more patience with David's obsessive-compulsive behaviors now that we saw him only on weekends and vacations. But his actions grated on us more than usual.

Sometimes after he'd acted inappropriately, he'd apologize: "I'm sorry—I'm smart. I'll learn. I'll do it right."

All week, he continued to wear his shoes in the house, glancing at us warily.

The day before we left for home, David came down from the loft, smiling. "I like to be a clown." I looked at him in confusion.

Then I remembered: Halloween was a month away. I saw him with his red plastic nose held onto his thin face with a brown rubber band; his shiny, bouffant, yellow wig with light brown hair sticking out under it; and his red and white polka-dot cap.

This had been his Halloween costume for the past fifteen years. With it, he would be wearing his everyday jeans and a button-down collar blue plaid shirt.

I smiled back at David. The week had not been a total loss. He liked to be a clown.

22

Wind Paper
A Rare, Playful Moment

Behind our vacation house in Sunriver, tall ponderosas, lodge poles, and shimmery aspen surround a flat area of needles and bunchgrass. The lack of fences, hedges, and clumpy shrubs means we can see into our neighbors' back yards. For many years, our next-door neighbor fed the deer in spite of warnings from the Nature Center they would never learn to forage for themselves. We enjoyed watching deer come and go from the feeder.

As usual, I sat in a canvas director's chair half-under the slatted wood canopy behind our house. Next door, a doe and two fawns chewed what looked like bird seed. Brown deck boards warmed the soles of my bare feet. A sudden breeze shook the aspens and moved on. I wrote in slanted cursive on a journal in my lap, *Gentle sounds: a door closing, a mourning dove's whoo, a grasshopper's rasp.*

David came from inside the house and sat next to me, looking out at the scene. "I like this beautiful day," he said in his monotone. Since he usually refers to himself as *you,* I took this as a subtle attempt to mind-read: I, Mom, like this beautiful day. That's why I'm sitting here.

"I just love the outside, huh? I like the weather, yeah I do." Maybe he *was* talking about himself.

A deer ran toward the river. "Run away, deer."

A newspaper page blew off the small table. "Wind paper." I quit writing about the beautiful day and started jotting down his comments, more poetic than usual.

"I hear the wind calling." He was keyed into the wind.

"I like the wind, too," I said. For once, we were sharing our deepest feelings.

As far as I could remember, David had only talked about wind twice before. The first time was when the two double-trunk maples plummeted in our yard in Portland. "We'll stop the wind," he'd insisted. The second time was when he and I had walked to our house from the beach in Manzanita. One block back from the ocean, he'd said, "No wind." I imagined he was wondering, *Why?* After thirty years of visiting the beach every few weeks or months, had he just noticed that strong winds abate when blocked by trees and houses?

In his late twenties, David began stringing words together as adjectives: "Want to go to the brown Oak Hills lunch-dinner restaurant." (He wanted to eat at the Oak Hills McMenamin's.) "Building a new road-crossing street." (He'd noticed the new road at the bottom of our hill.) These were attempts to explain. But his phrase *wind paper* seemed playful. So did his statements "I hear the wind calling" and "Run away, deer." These expressions were far removed from "Mom will make chicken for dinner," his usual level of conversation.

I looked at the glistening leaves and needles in our clearing. Was it any surprise they might create a pocket of sunlight in us? Too often, David was forced to live in a place his mind made for him. This time he had made his own space, and it was light as wind.

23

Where Do We Need to Be?
The Enigma of Home

When David and my mother-in-law accompanied us on trips, Phil drove and Jean sat in the front passenger seat next to him. David claimed his usual spot on the right side in the back and I sat beside him. That pleased everyone. Phil's mom could look at the scenery and visit with her son, David didn't bother his father with occasional loud talk, and I could read and drowse.

In late September 2004, the four of us drove home from Sunriver on Highway 20. The white peaks of the Three Sisters loomed to our left. Tall ponderosas with russet bark stood in groves. Wood fences surrounded fields with well-kept barns and sleek horses.

As we drove through the town of Sisters and continued northwest, David was quiet, looking straight ahead or out his window. Before we turned onto Highway 22, a mix of pines and Douglas fir replaced ponderosas and lodge-poles. Vine maples flamed against the green backdrop. Construction workers in orange vests with yellow reflective tape re-routed traffic into one lane.

Following the swift Santiam River, we came to Fishermen's Bend, a park with campsites, boat ramps, and trails hidden in trees along the river. I'd seen the sign many times and wished we could stop, but we always continued to Sunriver, or home to Portland. This time, I realized how much I liked the name Fishermen's Bend, a name that implied ownership and sounded welcoming.

David propped his left elbow on the overnight case between us, his chin resting on his palm, and looked at me. "Which house do we need to be into?" His language snapped me out of my reverie. I thought about his question—its weird construction, ending with the preposition *into;* its use of *we,* instead of *I;* and its inexplicable use of *need.*

I decided he was confused about whether he would return to our house or to his group home. It had been three years since he'd moved, but maybe he was still adjusting to the change. Or maybe he didn't know which house we would go to first.

"We're taking you to your house—89th Court. Then Dad and Grandma and I will go to our house." I wasn't sure I'd answered his question, but he seemed satisfied. He looked ahead, through the space between the front seats.

I kept turning over David's question, "Which house do we need to be into?" When I'd returned home from the writers' workshop at Linfield College seven years before, David hadn't relaxed until the clock radio and Dodge minivan were in their proper places.

Returning them was essential to his sense of order and stability. He trusted now that we would take him to the right house. The word "need" had an air of inevitability.

But the pronoun *we* invited a larger frame. Phil and I would soon move to Manzanita, a small town on the Oregon coast, where we would make a new home. It was where we wanted to be in retirement, where I thought I needed to be. The ocean, with its sandy beach, satisfied my yearnings. Where did David *need* to be? What constituted *home* for him? What yearnings might he have?

I'd liked the name "Fishermen's Bend" because it suggested ownership in a place. That's what I was looking for. Maybe David wanted the same thing.

I was working at my desk when David came into the office and sprawled on the blue carpet behind me. I turned to see him gazing at a family photo collage propped against the wall. That afternoon I'd left it on the floor, intending to hang it later.

His long legs tucked behind him, David leaned close to the photos of himself and his brother and sister when they were young. "I like to swing. I'll get my suitcase and go. I won't get my shoes too dirty for that carpet. I'll take my shoes off."

I looked at him, stunned. What made him think he could go back in time? I knelt next to him on the floor. Oh yes, I remembered that picture. David, seven, looked down smiling as his grandfather pushed him on a homemade swing—a board hung by two ropes from a willow tree. The green lawn didn't look muddy. Did David always take his shoes off before he went inside? I couldn't remember.

I studied the picture of the two-story house my father built evenings and weekends after working at the shoe factory, the yard where I'd played, the willow tree that had gotten a disease and had to be cut down. It seemed we *could* go there, even though years ago my parents had moved to a smaller place in Scappoose, the carpet David vowed to keep clean had been replaced by new owners, and my father had recently died.

Even as an adult, David often thought he could go back to a favorite school or ride in a child-sized car or train. This time, his longing didn't seem foolish; it matched my own: The house in the photograph was the place I'd fed the rabbits before school, played hide-and-seek in the cornstalks, picnicked and built forts in the woods. It was where my two brothers, sister, and I gathered as adults with our families for holidays and birthdays and where David usually stayed when Phil and I went away for a weekend. Where David ran on the large lawn and splashed in the hot tub and where his grandmother filled the house with smells of beef stroganoff and chocolate cake and his grandfather held him on his knee and belted out, "She'll be comin' 'round the mountain when she comes."

My throat tightened as I went back to my desk.

On a sunny fall day a few years later, I walked from my mother's new duplex apartment in Scappoose to J.P. West Road and up the hill. My breath came faster as the road climbed. Suddenly I was six, walking home from school, counting telephone poles until I got to Grandma and Grandpa's house. I checked the snapdragons I'd planted in the yard, went inside, and reached into the white cookie jar in the kitchen near the wood stove. The sugar cookie I pulled out had a few lumps and ragged edges, unlike the even, round cookies my mother made, but it tasted just as good. I told Grandma about what had happened at school that day and then continued on my way home.

As I climbed the same hill now, the grassy fields dotted by a few small houses had been replaced by large housing developments. I turned onto Keys Road. A woman weeded a row of dahlias in front of the house where I'd babysat four young boys, reading to them for hours to keep them corralled.

Finally, I came to our family's former home. The field and woods below it had long ago been sold for a housing development. The apple, pear, walnut, and fig trees; vegetable garden and strawberry patch; rabbit hutches, cow shed, and forts of my childhood were gone. Yet, the stalwart, gray two-story house with an inviting front porch—old-fashioned but well cared for—remained, surrounded by expensive modern homes.

The double-hung wood windows had been replaced with stylish new ones, the detached garage joined to the house by a covered walk, and the hot tub David loved removed. But my father's red brick barbecue still stood behind the house. Someone had even completed the upstairs bedrooms he roughed in but never had time to finish.

The house lived on, recognizable and in good condition, a tribute to both my father and the current owners. I imagined asking the people who lived there if David and I could visit.

We'd take off our shoes before we went inside.

24

Special Olympics Skiing
Lost Opportunities

After David moved to the group home, he could participate in Special Olympics cross country skiing only if he stayed at our house on the weekends he had practice, since the home didn't have a staff member to take him to his bus and pick him up at the end of the day. Dry land training usually began in December, with practices at Mt. Hood Meadows each weekend in January and February and final games at Mt. Bachelor the first weekend of March.

Over the sixteen years David took part in the program, Phil and I worked out a system: Phil did the morning run, driving David to the Fred Meyer parking lot in Beaverton at 6:00 a.m. for the bus trip to the mountain, and I did the evening run, picking him up at 5:30 p.m. Though I didn't have to venture out early on a cold, dark morning, I often waited more than an hour for the bus in the evening because it was stuck in traffic coming back from the mountain. Now that David lived in Tualatin, I had to drive him back to 89th Court after practice, too.

On Sunday mornings, David got up with a single wake-up call and pulled on long underwear, turtleneck, bibs, and wool socks. He clomped around the house in his ski boots, unwilling to wait to put them on until it was time to leave. Phil checked off items in his duffel bag: wool cap, gloves, sunglasses, handkerchief, an extra set of clothes, sunscreen, water, snacks, sack lunch, spending money, and lunch-time medications. David picked up his skis and poles from the kitchen floor, where he'd laid them the night before, and loaded them into the minivan.

Half-way through the season, the coaches timed everyone. We watched David plow into a fellow skier on a slight slope because he couldn't judge how to miss her. "D-a-a-v-i-i-d," she yelled. I wondered how many people he'd run into during his skiing life.

The Winter Games in March were a social event as much as an athletic one. Participants took dress-up clothes for a dinner and dance on Saturday night. On Sunday afternoon, they waited in front of a large judges' stand for their ribbons and medals. Though David lacked the competitive spirit and needed prodding to pass anyone, he usually picked up two medals. His long legs put him at an advantage, especially against athletes with Down syndrome.

Each year before the Winter Games, the coaches held an evening meeting during the week to go over the schedule and announce what the athletes should bring to the event. After David moved to 89th Court, I thought we might skip this meeting. He didn't seem to care whether he went or not, and information didn't change much from one year to the next. Why couldn't I just read the hand out? Then I wouldn't have to drive to Tualatin during rush hour, pick David up and take him to the Rec Center, drive him home, and then drive myself home. But his coach wanted him there. I knew volunteers gave up so much of their time for the athletes; this was the least I could do.

Before the 2002 meeting for the Winter Games, David led the way into the Cedar Hills Rec Center. Jimmy, another man from the cross country team and a former classmate of David's, showed us the right room. After waiting for everyone to filter in, Laurie, the cross country coach, herded a dozen participants and a few parents around a long table. I sat down next to David.

"Do you have any questions?" Laurie looked at us from the opposite end of the long table.

"Stay in Sunriver?" David asked in a clear, commanding voice. I hadn't even thought he was listening.

"No, David." Laurie's tone suggested he always asked questions. "We stayed in Sunriver when you went with us two years ago, but this year we're staying at a motel in Bend."

Silently, I thanked her for her patient response. David had already heard where they were staying from the assistant coach and from me, but he wanted Laurie's verification. He was disappointed they weren't staying in Sunriver. The lodge there had hosted the Winter Games for years, holding an elegant banquet and dance and allowing athletes to use the swimming pool and hot tub. The hot tub was especially important to David. But these luxuries ended two years before. Now the dinner and dance were in Bend.

I was proud of David for asking his question: It was an attempt at communication and an assertion of his rights. Too often, he simply accepted his fate as if he thought, *This is the way it is for me. I can't do anything to change it.* He'd expressed his desire to go back to Sunriver the only way he could, even if he already knew Laurie's answer wouldn't be the one he wanted.

The year Phil and I moved to the beach ended David's participation in Special Olympics cross country skiing. With reluctance, we told the coach there was no one to take him to practices. Another parent offered, but the drive from her house would have been difficult for her, and the group home staff couldn't help David get ready so early in the morning.

We hoped he might get to ski a weekend or two each year, but that never happened. We thought, too, that taking part in Special Olympics bowling would soften the blow, but it never did. "Go skiing?" David asked in the fall the first few years after we moved to the beach. Then he quit asking.

His skis and poles remain at the back of a closet in our basement so he won't see them when he visits—and we won't see them either.

25

The Lure of Food and Drink
"Extreme Food and Liquid Seeking"

David climbed out of our Honda and dashed ahead of me into my mother's trim duplex apartment. He hung up his jacket and raced toward the kitchen without looking at his grandmother. While I said hello, he lifted the head from the brown chicken-shaped cookie jar on the counter. With his back to us, he ate a homemade chocolate chip cookie, dropping crumbs on the vinyl floor.

"David, did you say hi to Grandma?"

"Hi, Grandma," he mumbled through a full mouth.

"It's all right," my mother said. "This is why he likes to come here." Her voice sounded resigned but sad she couldn't have the relationship with David she had with her other grandchildren.

"It's not the only reason he likes to come," I protested, but I worried she might be right. David often said, "Grandma cooks good food." Though she understood why he didn't look at her, talk to her, or give her hugs, I could see why she might think he cared more about her food than about her. He'd written in his high school literacy booklet that his best friend was Grandma and had drawn her in a purple dress with clodhopper shoes. But if he thought of her as a friend, he didn't show it.

David treated his sister, Lisa, in much the same way. She grimaced with sadness—and perhaps resentment—whenever David said, "Lisa makes good brownies" because she recognized he wanted her to make more. Unfortunately, he showed more interest in her brownies than in her. If he had shown he cared about her, his comment might have brought a smile.

Soon after David visited his grandmother, he stayed at our house a few days. While he was there, he made repeated trips to the kitchen to check out the food and drink, and to grab a snack. When I found him standing in the pantry once again, I said with more than a trace of sarcasm, "David, do you live in the pantry?" He didn't answer right away, but a couple minutes later he came into the living area and declared, "Mom, I don't live in the pantry." He hadn't realized I was joking.

David's weight was normal, but I worried his huge consumption of food and drink would affect his health. What had caused his increased eating, and how should we deal with it?

Part of the problem was David's obsessive-compulsive behavior. He would finish a box of cereal not because he was hungry, but so he could crumple the box and recycle it. The matter had spiraled out of control. In the spring of 2010, he ate a whole gallon of ice cream and drank all the orange juice, pop, and milk in our refrigerator in one weekend—enough food for three people. What's more, he wouldn't listen to suggestions about cutting back. His determination to eat and drink what he wanted, in the amounts he wanted, caused tension during his visits.

In our previous house, David often got a bag of nuts or a can of pop from the garage, but his eating and drinking were within reasonable limits. In our newly remodeled beach house, the pantry, immediately off the kitchen, lent itself to browsing. A bright light and white shelves set off the colorful labels on bottles and cans. The organization—cereal, crackers, and other boxed items on the left, cooking and baking supplies in the middle, and soups and canned vegetables on the right— no doubt appealed to David's need for structure. His rapt attention as he looked at the well-stocked shelves reminded me of my own pleasure when I gazed at a row of books. He ran his hand along the boxes with the same satisfaction I felt when I evened the spines of my favorite titles.

In the group home, food and drink were locked up because of David's obsessions and those of a housemate. The other resident persuaded David, who was tall enough to reach the key, to get into the locked food cupboard. While I abhor locking up food, I remember a friend's son swigging Coke from a two liter bottle at a picnic years ago. His mother said staff at his group home allowed residents to shop at a neighborhood grocery store without supervision. Her son gained an alarming amount of weight. I understood why David's staff took preventative steps to stop residents from eating and drinking too much. Yet, denying access only increased the attraction for residents.

The excessive consumption of food and drink became an even greater problem after David began taking Depakote and later Zyprexa, mood stabilizers meant to relieve his bipolar symptoms but which increased appetite and thirst. "Extreme food seeking" and "extreme liquid seeking" were added to his behavioral risk factors in 2009. When I discussed the matter with the Rehab Manager at his workplace, she mentioned that other workers on Depakote stole from co-workers' lunchboxes because they were so hungry.

Beverages, especially, became a control issue. At work, David downed the last drops from pop cans in the recycling bin and wouldn't stop when staff directed him to return to work. He insisted on drinking cup after cup of coffee with a generous lacing of cream and sugar. He asserted his independence in the one area where he had control.

Not only did David's compulsive eating and drinking affect his life at home and at work, but they limited his social activities, too. The group home staff could no longer take him to church because he made too many trips to the refreshment table after the service. His housemate's brother asked that David not come along on visits because David drank all the pop in the refrigerator. Relatives recoiled when he ate all the sausage and cheese on the appetizer tray at a family party.

We don't want to deny David the pleasure of eating, but we need to balance his need for personal choice with his need to be healthy. With a limited connection to others and few leisure skills, he's especially vulnerable to substituting food and drink for other activities. Since he can't monitor his own eating and drinking, we need to provide opportunities for exercise and recreation and help him to make good food choices. We don't want him to live in the pantry.

26

The New Jacket
Fixation on Familiar Objects

In his thirties, David often became attached to a particular article of clothing. For many weeks, he wore only a long-sleeved blue dress shirt with the same pair of jeans. Without redirection, he wore the same set of underwear, too. Keeping his clothes clean and replacing anything worn out was a challenge for group home staff and for us.

Once, when David visited Phil and me, I noticed on our walk to the beach that his jacket didn't close over his small pot belly. After we got home, I took the jacket out of the closet to see what was wrong. The zipper had several missing teeth and wouldn't engage. What's more, the object was old and dingy. As I tried to get the zipper to work, David stood near me, guarding his jacket as if afraid I'd send it to the reject pile. He knows me too well.

"The zipper's broken," I announced.

"It's not broken." He rescued his jacket and hung it in the closet.

That evening, I suggested to Phil that before taking David home on Friday, we go to the Columbia Sportswear outlet store in Woodburn to get him a new jacket: "We'll be back before dark." It was a two-hour drive to Tualatin, another half-hour to Woodburn. Phil groaned. I knew he wasn't thinking only of the trip but of the resistance we'd face.

"I don't want a new jacket," David repeated in the back seat as we headed to Woodburn in a driving rain. We parked in front of the shops and stood in a downpour at the village directory to find the location of the sportswear shop.

Inside the store, we immediately saw a jacket almost the same as the one David wore—blue, gray, and white. The zipper worked. The lining could be removed when the weather got warmer. Perfect.

"I don't want to try on the jacket," David said as I forced it over his shoulders. It was a better size for him than the old one, which hadn't been long enough. We were lucky to have found the new coat the minute we walked in the door.

"This one's good, isn't it, Phil?"

"Yup, it's good." He shot me a conspiratorial glance.

"No, it's not good! It's too big! It won't work!" David's anger escalated. He would do anything to avoid buying this piece of clothing. We had to get him out of the store quickly.

Phil paid for the purchase and shuttled David out the door. I stayed behind to check the racks of women's rain gear. I left moments later without buying anything, afraid of what I'd find in the car if I stayed longer.

When we got to the group home in Tualatin, David carried his red Nike duffel bag with his clothes inside while Phil waited in the car. In the house, I turned over David's new jacket to a young man from Ukraine who worked at the home on Fridays and weekends. He wrote David's initials on the label in black permanent ink, making the acquisition official.

I'd almost reached the door with the old jacket in the bag before David saw me, ripped the bag from my hand, and took it out. I grabbed it back. I wasn't going to give up now. David got hold of a sleeve. We moved toward the door as if dancing, both grasping the jacket. The young man on staff stood in the hallway, shaking his head.

In the driveway, David and I continued our tug of war, pulling on the slippery fabric until I thought it would rip. "I want it, I want it, I want it!" David shouted with a rare use of the word *I*. We stared into each other's eyes, our jaws set. Finally, I wrenched the jacket from David and he walked back in the house without a word.

Phil and I drove home, the old jacket in the back seat. Had the struggle been worth it? If I hadn't taken the jacket away, David would have kept wearing it for months, maybe years. But would that have mattered? Did it matter that the zipper didn't work? He could have kept using the snaps to close it, as he'd been doing. The old coat would have looked shabby when he went to work or on community outings. But would anyone have cared except me?

David's brain creates an image of how something should appear, and he gets upset if an item deviates from that image. But don't I also create a model of what I want and find it hard to deviate from it? Don't I also insist on control?

27

Making Things Happen
Advocating for Health Care and Daily Support

The year before David moved to a group home, he needed medical clearance to continue cross-country skiing with Special Olympics. I shepherded him into a small examination room at The Portland Clinic. The physician had been David's primary care doctor for the past ten years and also treated other members of our family. He entered the room, looked down at his clipboard, and glanced at David. "How's it going at Nike?"

"Tualatin Valley Workshop," I corrected him, surprised at his question. Did David look like a Nike employee? Then I remembered this doctor had another male patient with autism. Maybe that person worked at Nike. I couldn't fault a busy doctor for mixing up his patients. Or maybe he'd simply forgotten where David worked. At least, he'd addressed David directly instead of talking to him through me, as some doctors had done.

The physician took the Special Olympics form from my hand. It didn't seem to matter to him that he'd made a mistake about David's workplace. He asked me a few questions about David's health, filled out the check list on the form, signed it, handed it to me, and turned to walk away. We'd waited two months for this appointment, and I expected him to ask me to leave the room so he could give David a physical exam.

I quickly explained some of my concerns: David's knuckles were calloused and cracked. He didn't wash his hands well, and I worried the cracks would become infected. I wondered if the lipomas—benign, fatty tumors—on his arms and back could be caused by the psychotropic medications he'd begun taking. The doctor brushed aside each concern. We were out of his office in fifteen minutes.

The issues I'd brought up were relatively small, but what if David had something seriously wrong? I don't think this doctor would have caught it. What if Phil and I weren't looking out for David? Could we ever *not* be looking out for him?

When I mentioned our experience to David's psychiatrist, he said he and his mental health colleagues were very concerned about the lack of thorough physical exams their patients received from their primary care doctors. He cited the case of a woman patient who was severely autistic, who couldn't speak and rocked back and forth. She hit her head on the back of the bathtub while rocking and was taken to her primary care doctor. Instead of examining her, the doctor didn't even touch her. According to the psychiatrist, when the woman came to him for her next appointment, she had "raccoon eyes," the sign of a skull fracture. He called her primary care doctor to report his finding.

"I'm afraid to go on vacation anymore," he said. "Afraid of how many patients I will have lost by the time I get back." He felt certain a patient had recently died from cancer that had gone undiagnosed because his physician didn't catch the warning signs, and the psychiatrist had not been there to advocate. An article in our local newspaper later corroborated his claim that people with developmental disabilities received inferior medical care.[11]

Simple guidelines suggest the primary care doctor should treat the person and family member or other caregiver with respect—look each person in the eye and call him or her by name, maintain a working relationship with the patient's other doctors, and check the same things he would check for a person without developmental disabilities.

The treatment David received at The Portland Clinic that day made me feel he didn't count as a person. I worried he received inferior treatment because he couldn't answer the doctor's questions, and the doctor couldn't relate to him. On the other hand, I should have asked beforehand how long the appointment would be. If I didn't think the allotted time was long enough, I could have said, "We need a longer appointment." In addition, I could have asked for an earlier appointment. By late afternoon, patients had piled up in the waiting room and the doctor was rushed.

In the end, good advocacy depends upon being persistent enough to get the answers you need.

Good advocacy also requires weighing benefits and risks. Even medical testing can have a dehumanizing effect on the patient. When David's head measurement was posted in the hallway during his evaluation at two years, when his neck vein was pricked to check for chromosome abnormalities a few weeks later, and when his testicles were measured to screen for Fragile X Syndrome at eighteen, I wondered if the procedures were a needless invasion of his humanity. Were they intended to benefit him or only to give us answers?

David's mental health care has raised other questions: When should one medicate to decrease problem behaviors and when should one use love and patience? What is the proper balance? Our experience has shown finding the right combination of medications to treat psychiatric disorders in a person with autism can be more an art than a science. The result is an ongoing search for the best—or least damaging—combination of drugs.

In addition to advocating for David's physical and psychological wellbeing in medical situations, Phil and I have represented his interests in his vocational and residential programs. Since he began work at age twenty-one, we've attended annual Individual Support Plan (ISP) meetings to determine his progress and set goals for his future.

The Individual Support Plan is a set of written agreements intended to help the person with developmental disabilities live a happy, meaningful life. It's usually about thirty-five pages but can be twice as long if there are also issues with physical or emotional conditions. As a legal document, it's the best tool family members and guardians have to ensure the person they care about is healthy and safe. But the ISP is only as effective as the team that creates and carries out specific goals.[12]

When David began working after high school, his ISP team consisted of Phil and me (his parents and legal guardians), his vocational program manager, and his county case manager, sometimes called a services coordinator, and himself. After he entered a group home, the residential program manager joined his ISP team, and our meeting time was split between reports from the vocational and residential managers. The Alternative-to-Employment program that replaced David's work program was also considered a vocational program, and the manager became part of the ISP team.

A few years ago, Oregon developed a person-centered ISP process. Step one was to gather information from the person and those who care about him or her and record the data on a Personal Focus Worksheet. The worksheet asked simple questions: What's important to the person? What does the person love to do? Who does the person like to see? What's happening that's working? What's happening that isn't working? What should be happening but isn't?

David's fourteen-page worksheet included statements from him and our family about what was important to him: *I get to go home, I get to see my family, I sit in my chair and watch tv, I listen to rap, I go to Sunriver, I go to Kiwanis Camp* . . . It also listed what he didn't like, such as being told what to do, what to eat or drink, and what to wear.

Under "Communication Needs," David's ISP advised staff, "David is very direct with his communication and likes to be very close to people when he is talking to them. He doesn't realize that his proximity may be too close for their personal space needs. Support David by gently reminding him when he is getting too close to somebody. He may also need to be reminded not to talk loud."

The ISP also identified significant health and safety risks using the Risk Tracking Record. David's record included "David's afraid of dogs and may cross the street or climb a fence to avoid them."

At a meeting about the new person-centered ISP process, an Oregon Technical Assistance Corporation representative said solemnly, "The ISP team's weighty task is to give voice to this person." I thought about David's housemate who couldn't speak at all, and about David himself, who could communicate only minimally. I thought about all the family members and nonprofit board members I'd known who devoted thousands of hours to helping people with disabilities. So many people give voice to those who can't speak for themselves.

Though the ISP team is required to meet yearly, anyone on the team can ask for a meeting during the year if they think one is needed. On our team, Phil and I have usually been the ones to call a special meeting because the other team members were busy with other clients. Often, we've been the ones to say, "Our plans aren't working." In spite of the elaborate ISP structure, if no one notices there's a problem and advocates, the system breaks down. As with health care, it's those who care the most who must make things happen.

28

Uncle Billy's Magic Hammer
The Need for Motivation

Phil tells a story about perseverance in spite of a disability. When he was a child, his family visited his aunt and uncle on the east side of Portland. Inside their house, the grownups and kids stood around a bedroom closet his Uncle Billy had just lined with cedar.

"M-m, doesn't that smell good?" The grownups admired the red and cream-colored wood.

His grandfather winked at him. "How do you think Uncle Billy got those boards up there?"

With a hammer and nails, Phil thought. What a crazy question!

"But Uncle Billy only has one arm." His grandfather grinned.

Slowly it dawned on Phil. How could his uncle hold the nail and pound it at the same time?

Uncle Billy pulled a hammer and a bag of nails from the back of the closet, put a nail on the end of his hammer, and held the hammer head in the air. The nail stuck!

"Wow, how'd you do that?"

"The hammer's magnetized . . . See? Sometimes I have to ask Aunt Marian to hold the board. Otherwise, I do just fine."

This story is as much about Phil as about Uncle Billy. Phil came by hard work and building naturally. Growing up, he worked in his family's building supply business and returned after college to help his father run the business. His parents were self-reliant and taught him everyone must work to the best of his or her ability.

In his early thirties, Phil designed and built our beach house on weekends, often driving his company truck with wallboard and other supplies to our lot and unloading it after work on Fridays. Afraid of heights, he asked me to hold his feet while he dangled head-first to nail roofing near the eaves of our two-story house. Later, he fashioned a T-frame out of 2x4s for me to hold a sheet of wallboard against the ceiling while he nailed it in place. After we finished the wallboard work, he hoisted a dresser and several boards onto a table to make a platform for a heavy light fixture he wired into the kitchen ceiling. No obstacle was too great.

In a way, the story of Uncle Billy is David's story, too. If David hadn't been born with autism, he might have been much like Phil. As a toddler, he liked to pound wooden pegs through a board with a toy hammer, turn the board over, and pound the pegs back again. At six, he built houses with Lincoln Logs and drove nails into a weathered board. While Phil and I framed the beach house garage, he filled a crack between two studs with nails wedged together as closely as possible, creating a long platoon of steely heads. Like his father, he didn't think of construction as work, but as fun. He liked to see the result of his efforts.

But by the time David was in high school, a teacher commented he had "a little learned helplessness." I sensed a warning: If professionals and family members did too much for him, he would quit doing things for himself. As David has lost more and more motivation to work as an adult, I've wondered if his teacher wasn't clairvoyant.

Have we sometimes forgotten to let David do things himself, or failed to teach him as a parent must always teach a child? Have we stepped in too quickly because we could do the job better and faster? Probably. But the matter is more complex than this. David doesn't seem to see the importance of his work or to reap a sense of reward. Bipolar and obsessive-compulsive disorders in adulthood have made it hard for him to work, too. There is no magic hammer to fix this problem.

As David lost more and more motivation to work in his thirties, I wondered if we could find a job for him—even a volunteer job—in line with his interests, instead of trying to bend his interests to fit a mold. For a short period in his twenties, he'd helped me replace attendance cards and pencils in the pews at our church. In subsequent years, he asked every once in a while, "Do cards and pencils?" Apparently, he'd enjoyed this simple task. He liked to work with paper, and a repetitive job appealed to him. Unfortunately, our church had moved to an attendance tracking system that didn't require the use of cards and pencils. Now that he lived in a group home, he wouldn't have been available to help me replenish them anyway.

His work options were limited, too. The vocational provider had no collating work available, and by his middle thirties, David needed one-on-one staff to stay on task, a luxury his service payment didn't cover.

In the absence of better alternatives, David's psychiatrist searched for meds that would help him to focus and stay seated at his work program, and Phil and I partnered with vocational and group home staff to seek solutions to his increasing unwillingness and inability to work. We also tried to show David we valued him as a person, regardless of how much he accomplished. When it became clear David could no longer perform packaging jobs, we helped him move to an Alternative-to-Employment program, where he played games, put together puzzles, and went on community outings.

Though I understood David could no longer work, I felt he'd taken a step backward. I thought of motivational quotes I'd seen in classrooms: *No one can do everything, but everyone can do something . . . Your "I will" is more important than your IQ.* I remembered the motto athletes spoke at David's Special Olympics events: "Let me win, but if I cannot win, let me be brave in the attempt." I thought of David's words when he was twenty-six, "You make your own ham-cheese-pickle sandwich. You're doing pretty good!" I wished he could regain the sense of accomplishment he'd felt then.

David glanced at the message I'd written on a small notepad on our kitchen counter: *Sunset—Tuesday 10/26, 7-3:00.* After a moment he said, "Mom's going to Sunset High School like you did." Since he usually referred to himself as *you,* I knew he was remembering his own high school years at Sunset, which had ended eight years before. Did he think I was a student there?

In a way, I suppose I was.

When I'd started subbing a few years before, I'd assumed my work would be mainly in my subject area: language arts. But the greatest need for high school subs in our district was in special education. It didn't take long until one-third of my work days were in this field. Because I'd often visited David's classes and knew his friends and teachers, I felt comfortable in special ed settings. Classes were small and discipline rarely a problem. Something else may have guided me, too: Special ed gave me glimpses into David's former world, a world I was trying to understand and write about. As I traveled from school to school, I met one student who most exemplified the spirit of trying I wished David—and all of us—could acquire.

I found lesson plans in the office, flanked on one side by a one-way mirror so the teacher could keep an eye on the classroom as she plowed through mountains of paperwork. She was required by law to create an Individual Education Plan (IEP) for each student and to document progress for a long list of goals. Above her desk was a plaque with the inscription "To teach is to touch a life forever." In this class, where students had significant cognitive and physical disabilities, that was particularly true.

On the other side of the one-way glass, a middle-aged woman lifted a blond teenager in gray sweats out of his wheelchair and onto a floor mat. His body was thin and twisted with cerebral palsy, but he had fair, smooth skin and expressive blue eyes. The assistant lowered herself onto the mat next to him. "Reach, Joey, reach!" She extended the boy's right arm. His hand remained curled in a tight fist, his thumb locked between middle fingers. But he reached. In slow increments, the woman helped him stretch each arm and leg—perhaps an inch. The routine appeared familiar to the assistant and student, but to me it was anything but familiar.

As the day went on, Joey dropped bright-colored foam blocks into a bucket on the floor next to his wheelchair, cheering when he made a basket. He swatted a red button on a plastic tray attached to his chair to start "Robin in the Rain," a Raffi song. As the music played, he swayed in his chair to the beat. When a student aide in his classroom admonished, "Get that tongue in, Joey," he didn't make a face, as I would have; he smiled and tried to suck in his tongue.

That afternoon, Joey smiled at me as I wheeled him around in the warm sun at a park near the school. As we circled the grounds, he said a few words I recognized: "hi," "yeah," and "mo." "Mo, mo, mo" meant "more water." (His medications made him thirsty.) Joey couldn't do things most of us take for granted: walk, tie his shoes, carry on a conversation. But, at least on the day I spent in his classroom, he worked to the best of his abilities. His spirit glowed. He made everyone around him smile. He was reaching.

Why couldn't David do the same? Had autism robbed him not only of the ability to relate to others, but also of the ability to gain pleasure from his accomplishments?

I think of Joey and his teachers as examples of what special ed can be, what life should be for all of us: challenging and rewarding. Of course, not every special ed student is as happy as Joey. Some are frustrated because they're not accepted by their peers; some have given up because the work is hard, and they don't see it will improve their lives. And, though most teachers believe "to teach is to touch a life forever," the truth is some are burnt out. Another subbing assignment seemed to bear out these observations:

A green and white large-print Webster's School Dictionary normally used in elementary schools sat on the teacher's desk. Nearby, the tops of four file cabinets overflowed with a jumble of books and magazines, file folders and pencils, many chewed and lacking erasers. At the back of the room, two more file cabinets and a bookcase with nicked beige paint—the same color as the walls and speckled floor—held a world globe and a Red Vines plastic jar stuffed with more marking pens and pencils.

A strip of cursive letters with animal pictures corresponding to each sound and a multiplication table and a division chart intended for grade-schoolers flanked one wall. Jumbo crayons on a poster spelled "Welcome to Class . . . Learning is Fun." I shuddered. This classroom was not only drab and dirty, but it was also age-inappropriate. The few posters geared to high school students were discouraging. One warned, "Dropping out of school isn't the end of your problem. It's the beginning of a new and bigger one." Another advised, "Keep within your heart a place where dreams may grow." This isn't a place my dreams would grow, I thought, thankful David's classrooms had been cheerful.

The warning bell rang and I greeted students as they straggled in. My job was simple: to encourage everyone to work and to assign points at the end of the period based on productivity. This was a Resource Room study hall intended for students more able than David to learn academic skills. After roll, the classroom quieted down. One girl typed at a computer table along the wall. Four boys listened to music with headphones as they did homework, a practice the teacher allowed. Others worked quietly, their heads bent over their desks. Everyone was mellow, still waking up in this morning class.

One boy had his head on his desk as though he was sleeping. I went over to talk to him. "Do you have some work to do?"

He raised his head, yawned, and shrugged. "No."

As I looked into the boy's face, I recognized Ralph. A few months ago, he had proudly told me about learning Spanish and uttered a few words to prove it. Now, his frayed clothes didn't fit properly. His straw-colored hair looked uncombed. He opened his scratched binder: three empty metal rings, not a page of work.

"Last time I was here, you were learning Spanish."

He shrugged again. "I never learned any Spanish."

At the end of class, I wrote two points out of ten on Ralph's daily record sheet, giving him credit for showing up and bringing his binder. I started to pack my things to move to another room for the next class.

Ralph still sat at his desk, peering up at me through sleepy eyes. "Do you think you could help me? I'm fifteen cents away from lunch."

I knew the rule: Don't loan to students. Teachers worked hard to build self-reliance. But I picked up my teaching bag and told Ralph to follow me. I stopped in the office where I'd stowed my purse and took out two dimes; I didn't have a nickel. The truth was I felt sorry for Ralph. He lacked the right clothes, the right skills, and the right manner. I hope he went back to learning Spanish and filled his binder. I hope my small contribution to his lunch didn't increase his sense of helplessness.

These experiences taught me each person has unique abilities and challenges. There is no single magic hammer to inspire each of us to live life to the fullest. Joey and Ralph had disabilities, but their challenges were not the same. Their obstacles were different from David's, too. David has a unique set of characteristics that make work difficult for him. Because of his autism, parts don't always come together to make a whole. Repetitive thoughts and actions interfere with work. On top of this, he has the specter of mental illness.

Still, I'm hopeful that, with the help of our family and his vocational and residential providers, David may regain some of the satisfaction in work he once felt.

Phyllis Mannan

V.

"Whatever being quiet is,"
he mutters, spewing
other people's messages
like a skewed
answering machine,
his arms swinging wildly
as he powerwalks the house.

Phyllis Mannan

29

Frizzled
Anxiety, OCD, and Separation from Self

"Home, home, home," David chanted in the back seat as we drove west on Highway 26, studded tires making a rough ride. I squirmed in our Subaru's hard front passenger seat. "Tillamook Cheese Factory go, restaurant go, lighthouse telescope go . . ." David listed places at the coast he liked but was now too anxious to enjoy.

After his psychiatric appointment that morning, he begged to go home to the beach with us. Now, he seemed mired in the place he didn't want to be: "Group home, put clothes away, closet doors closed." He didn't see the bright January sun, the fir-feathered hills and sparkling creeks swollen with snow melt. Though we hadn't arrived at the beach yet, in his mind he'd already finished his visit and returned to his group home.

"Mom . . . Mom . . . Mom . . ." In the back seat, he asked where we'd eat dinner, which bedroom he'd sleep in, when he'd go back to work. He didn't say, "Dad . . . Dad." He knew Phil didn't have patience for his repeated questions.

I tried a gentle reminder: "David, we've already talked about this." I was losing patience, too.

Phil was silent as he drove. I knew he dreaded having David at our house again, dreaded his poor table manners and hygiene, his continual eating and chugging drinks; the food smears on the table, chairs, and towels; his new habit of urinating on the floor when he used the toilet. How could we remain loving toward David when his habits had become so disgusting?

I glanced at him over my shoulder. His brow wrinkled and smoothed in a quick succession of frowns. His nose quivered; his mouth opened and closed like a fish. It was as if he were bursting out of his skin. For years, I'd worried he would develop tardive dyskinesia, involuntary movements of the face caused by long-term use of tranquilizers. We'd begun to notice twitches the previous year. The movements had been much smaller and less frequent than now, and we'd hoped they were just signs of anxiety. David's doctor said they didn't look like the tics he'd seen in other patients with the disorder. And David had shown twitches from time to time even before he started taking tranquilizers. Now, however, the doctor said the twitches probably were tardive dyskinesia.

I thought the word "tardive" ("developing late") sounded like "retarded"—the root's the same. And this condition could also be irreversible. My pain felt old, as though it had been recycled.

When David began taking psychotropic drugs at twenty-six, he didn't understand why he was taking them. Once, when I doled out his meds, he said, "I'll feel better. I won't use up all the pills, okay?" I felt guilty as I handed him the bright-colored tablets, but I reassured myself they were necessary. During the previous year, David had been lost in repetitive talk and anxious pacing. He began crossing a busy street to throw paper over a fence at his workplace and was almost hit by a car. On medication, his anxiety and obsessive-compulsive behavior decreased. He was calm enough to converse, package gift wrap at his workplace, and go on Park and Recreation day-trips to Hagg Lake and Mt. Hood. We knew his meds had trade-offs. We gambled muscle twitches wouldn't be one of them.

After I thought about *tardive,* I remembered another word: *frizzled.* Scientists thought frizzled genes—receptors that wind seven times back and forth through the plasma membrane of a cell—might play a role in autism.[13] The word conjured pictures of badly permed hair, bacon sputtering grease in a frying pan, a person struck by lightning. What's more, I'd read the gene activated a protein called "disheveled." I didn't know the science but figured "frizzled" must be a bad gene. The word seemed to describe David now. As we drove west on Highway 26, he was frizzled, and we were, too.

Three days later, Phil and I dropped David off at his home in Tigard and headed back to the beach with a mixture of relief and regret. Half-way home, we stopped at Elderberry Inn, a truck stop that delivered plain food at a modest price.

"Sit wherever you want," Virginia called out. A friendly waitress from the nearby town of Jewell, she always made us feel welcome. After Virginia took our order, I noticed a young man slumped sideways in his wheelchair near the window. He looked dazed, his eyes fuzzy, as the others at his table looked on quietly. From my experience in special ed classrooms, I realized he'd had a seizure.

"He just needs time to come back to himself," a woman—apparently his mother— reassured onlookers. I felt a connection with these people I didn't know. We could have been in their place, except David had been spared seizures. When he was with us, we considered restaurants carefully. The ideal place had a medium noise level, loud enough to cover up his occasional earsplitting comments, but not loud enough to trigger even louder talking; a clientele more family-oriented than trendy; and a staff who wouldn't be put off by his inability to decide what to order and his need for a half-dozen extra napkins. But we'd never had to worry he'd have a seizure or that there wouldn't be space at the table for a wheelchair.

After we left the restaurant, I thought about the words "He just needs time to come back to himself." In spite of his cognitive deficits, David had a core set of qualities—good humor, love of food and good times, and resilience—that made him a unique person. Lately, those core qualities had been under attack from within.

The previous week the lead staff at his home had lamented, "I feel like David's gone." I knew what she meant. He'd become so wrapped up in repetitive talk that he couldn't respond, couldn't share his simplest thoughts. I wanted to place my hands on his head, smooth his quivering brow, and return him to himself.

Later, as I walked on the beach, several large groups of seagulls stood at water's edge, facing into the wind. In each flock, a few birds flew southward and returned, their breasts shining like whitecaps. Their pattern of leaving and returning gave me hope, as if it signaled the restoration of a natural order in our human affairs, too. Could David's good humor and resilience be restored? Could he return to us? For the moment, I felt the answer to both questions was yes.

A few days after we drove David home, we got a phone call from him. We'd asked staff at his residence to encourage him to call so he would know he could get in touch with us if he felt lonely or had a problem. He didn't like to use the phone, but it was important he knew he could communicate with us, especially now that we lived two hours away. A staff member had been coaching him to use the correct phone number. He still wanted to punch in our old number, though it had been two years since it had changed.

David didn't say hello when he came on the phone. "No work," he pleaded. "Don't want to go to work."

"Why don't you want to go to work?" I said in my most sympathetic voice. I hoped he would answer, but "why" questions are hard for him.

"Don't want to go to work," he repeated.

I asked him about staff and what he'd been doing at work, but he didn't answer. I asked if he'd gone to a movie or Tuesday Treasures, a Christian function he enjoyed—anything to get his mind off work. But he said again, "No work." His plea had previously been mild and intermittent; now it was a mantra.

"I love you, David."

"Don't want to talk anymore." He hung up, unable to say what was wrong at work.

For the past eight years, he'd worked at Edwards Enterprises in Beaverton, a suburb of Portland. One of more than one hundred and thirty clients, as the workers are called, he assembled water and first aid kits, packaged holiday gift bags, and did an assortment of other packaging jobs. Projects were subcontracted from local businessmen, and clients earned a paycheck based on their productivity.

David had never earned much. In 2007, his highest productivity rate for a single month, based on what an average worker without disabilities would likely accomplish, had been four percent. Like many others with autism, he didn't seem to see a connection between his efforts and the finished product, and a paycheck meant little because he didn't want to buy anything. But he stayed at his work table and told staff about family gatherings, Park and Recreation District day trips, and Special Olympics cross country skiing. His occasional complaint, "No work," was of the "Gee, I don't want to go back to work on Monday" variety, but now he was insistent.

I've tried to pinpoint when David began doing less work at Edwards. In April, 2007, just before Phil and I moved to the beach, Edwards' Rehabilitation Manager rated David favorably on a scale of 5 as "always" and 1 as "never:"

- Works cooperatively: 4
- Can work continuously, without prompting for:
  A. 10 minutes: 5
  B. 20 minutes: 4
  C. 30 minutes: 3

- Independently produces acceptable quality of work or product: 4

- Initiates communication when:
  A. Work completed or out of material: 5
  B. Needs assistance: 5
  C. Mistake is made: 5
  D. Too sick or tired to work: 5
  C. Needs to use the restroom, get a drink, etc.: 5

She noted, however, "David may need cues to stay in his seat during work time."

By April 2009, things changed. The manager wrote in her yearly report, "David seems very anxious and on most days within the last three to four months has not been able to stay seated and work. He bursts into the building in the morning, really hyped, and begins moving around, straightening things. He never looks settled."

How would it be to never feel settled? I wondered.

We'd been hearing about problems at the workplace since November of the previous year. A pile of incident reports from staff indicated David wandered between the office area, restroom, and lunch room, moving pages on calendars, rearranging papers on staff desks, pushing down trash in garbage cans, and drinking remaining pop from cans in the recycling box.

One lead staff complained, "He takes the pen from my hand as I'm writing and relocates it to another desk. Once, he moved a trash can in the Health and Safety area as a coworker was trying to vomit into it." Not only did David not work, he kept others from working.

Another problem involved bus passes. For years, David hadn't wanted his co-workers to wear their passes around their necks. In his mind, a pass belonged in one's pocket. Now his behavior escalated. He got up while eating lunch and walked behind a woman sitting at another table. He stood staring at the back of her neck where a thick string under her shirt held her bus pass. He touched the back of her neck as if to untie the string. The woman screamed, alarming others in the lunch room. Staff asked David not to touch the woman and he walked away. But on other occasions, he walked behind her at her work station and stared at the back of her neck. Each time, staff cued him to return to his work area and he complied.

By July 2009, David's obsession about passes worsened. A supervisor wrote in an incident report, "While entering the bathroom, David attempted to remove B.K.'s bus pass from around his neck. Although staff redirected David to please use the other bathroom, he attempted to enter the bathroom three or four more times while B.K. was there and did not stop trying to get the bus pass until staff removed it and put it out of sight."

We looked for solutions to these problems. David's plea "No work" seemed to argue for a change of vocational programs, but his county case manager said there were no other appropriate programs nearby, and we were afraid a move from the Portland area would be harder for him than staying in his present situation. His psychiatrist tinkered with his meds, hoping to find a dosage and combination that would alleviate his anxiety and obsessive-compulsive behavior. We sought a second opinion on his meds without success.

By 2009, David's obsessive-compulsive disorder worsened in his group home, too. He frequently walked into a neighbor's yard to adjust his garden gnomes and flag. Even worse, he looked inside another neighbor's mail box to check for mail. Fortunately, both neighbors knew he had disabilities and didn't call the police.

To some extent, David had always been preoccupied with paper and with how objects should appear. A few years before, he'd walked up to the altar during a church service to rearrange the envelopes in the offering plate. The minister looked surprised when David began to rifle through the cash and envelopes, but he continued with the service. I think David noticed when the plate was passed in our pew that some of the envelopes were face-down. He was always careful to ensure our envelope landed with the printing on top. After the service, a man joked David must have needed some cash. I knew nothing was farther from his mind than taking money from the offering plate.

Now, David's compulsions skyrocketed. On community outings, he began to take other people's food or drink. We were shocked to hear he'd stolen a little girl's birthday cake and eaten part of it before staff could stop him. At his work site, he poured himself coffee from the staff office while the coffee was still brewing—a safety hazard as well as a breach of etiquette. If anyone left a drink unattended at home, at work, or in the community, it was fair game. Staff tried to redirect David, but he ignored their cues. "It's okay," he said as he swallowed the drink. How much of this behavior resulted from obsessive-compulsive disorder and how much from his medications, which caused excessive hunger and thirst, we didn't know.

Other behaviors became risk factors, too. David put his hands in the trash to rip up items and stuff them to the bottom of the can. He didn't always wash his hands afterward and didn't consider there might be dangerous items in the trash. The residential staff was instructed to be certain sharp objects were put into the recycling bin or the outside garbage can instead of in the kitchen garbage. The vocational staff was to be certain David washed his hands thoroughly before returning to his work table. As David spent more and more time washing his hands, he accomplished even less work.

The bottom line was that David now needed more staff support than ever before. Residential staff was told to "Provide constant verbal feedback. Know what is planned for the day, which staff will be working with David and when, what meals are planned, and what David has to look forward to during the coming week." These were the issues that occupied David's mind, but did an overworked staff have the time and energy to provide constant feedback?

David's obsessive trash compacting posed a particular problem for our family when we took him into the community. One afternoon, Phil and I picked him up at his workplace for a psychiatric appointment. His psychiatrist, one of few in the Portland area who accepted Medicaid patients, treated people with mental illness, and little or no personal income, with kindness.

When we arrived at the clinic, located in an old house, David strode toward the single restroom in the back. It had become his habit to visit the bathroom immediately after entering any home or business establishment—not to use the facilities but to push down the paper towels in the waste container. Phil headed toward the waiting room, and I followed David to encourage him to join us.

As David approached the restroom, a young woman walked ahead of him. He hurried past her, almost stepping on her heels.

"David, stop!" I called out.

As the woman stood with her hand on the knob, he pushed the door open and barged into the bathroom.

Again, I shouted, "David!" He disappeared behind the door.

The woman entered the restroom and stood with her back to the sink, looking out into the hall. She appeared dazed. "I've been waiting a long time," she said in a resigned voice. It seemed her life was full of uncontrollable events.

"I'm sorry," I said. "David, come out of the bathroom."

Paper rustled behind the door. The room was too small for three people, so I waited for the woman to move. Finally, she budged a few inches, and I could enter far enough to see David bent over, pushing down wet paper towels in a metal trash can.

As I stood feeling helpless, Phil came, grabbed David by the arm, and pulled him from the room.

The woman gazed at me with a sad expression and closed the door.

I didn't know her situation, but her plaintive appeal for David to leave made his actions all the more upsetting. I felt ashamed and embarrassed by his behavior. A year before, he would have stopped walking when I asked him to stop. He would have waited his turn if another person was entering a restroom. Now, he didn't heed my words or acknowledge boundaries.

He was beyond my control.

A behavioral specialist hired to help David pointed out his anxiety and increased obsessive-compulsive disorder were probably a delayed reaction to changes in staff and housemates, and to our move to the coast in 2007. David needs to know people are in their proper place; they're not supposed to move away. The behavior specialist wrote an assessment but stopped short of creating a behavior plan. She said David's home lacked adequate staff to implement a plan, and she couldn't write one for the vocational site since she'd been hired by the residential provider. We held meeting after meeting, but nothing changed. As David's unhappiness and troublesome behavior continued into 2010, we worried his behaviors were becoming ingrained.

In February, the new manager at 89th Court said, "David talks constantly about Nyamu bringing his truck to get the overnight bags to go to the beach. That conversation goes on for hours every night." David's fantasy surprised me because Nyamu had never brought him to our house for an overnight visit, and as far as I knew, David had never made up a story this elaborate before. Evidently, he wanted the trip to happen so much he talked as though it *would* happen.

I felt frustrated we hadn't been able to find a solution to David's situation. His thoughts and actions caused him grief and disturbed the people around him. I felt guilty Phil and I could live as if nothing had changed—walking on the beach, gardening, talking to friends—while David's life was in shambles and those entrusted with his care were left to pick up the pieces.

David was living in a cocoon of uncertainty and fear. He paced and talked loudly to himself much of the time. What would happen next week . . . tomorrow . . . in two minutes? Any event could be a tsunami, overturning his natural order. He was unable to live in the present, unable to appreciate what he saw, heard, tasted, and touched.

When I talked to him on the phone one Sunday, he cleared his throat, made moaning sounds and hung up. I called back to talk to staff and found he'd paced until 2:00 a.m. the night before. "He can't talk to me anymore," the lead staff said. Anxiety and obsessive-compulsive disorder seemed to have erased what limited ability he'd previously had to express his feelings. As a child and young adult, he'd trusted we would take care of him. For the first seven years in the group home, he'd felt comfortable and trusted staff. Now he seemed alone in his distress, and we couldn't comfort him.

One day, as we drove David home from a visit at our house, he kept leaning forward from the back seat to peer around Phil's right shoulder. He seemed interested in something on the steering wheel or dashboard. Suddenly, he reached between the two front seats.

"No, David!" I warned. Seeing his hand so close to the steering wheel wrenched my attention away from the book I was reading. Lately, we couldn't trust David. He'd changed so much. He used to be calm and predictable; now we didn't know what he would do.

He sat back against the upholstered seat. "Pull the hand hair?"

What did he say? I looked at Phil's hand, draped over the wheel. A few scraggly, gray-blond hairs sprang like wires from the back of it. In the bright sun, those Lilliputian hairs must have seemed like giants to David. How long had he been fighting the temptation to yank them out?

As David's OCD worsened, he became more concerned with getting rid of things that didn't belong: gravel kicked onto the asphalt at the side of the road, lint on a stranger's jacket, a piece of paper on the wrong stack at his home or workplace. He no longer respected boundaries. He moved his housemates' belongings around their rooms and dispatched staff reports to drawers or stuffed them between other papers. When the home's van was broken for weeks and residents and staff couldn't leave, tensions increased. For David and others at 89th Court, outings came second only to eating.

More and more, compulsive behaviors took over David's life. To help group home staff imagine what might be going through his mind and to increase their empathy, David's residential case manager-advocate wrote the following scenario. I think it's as close as anyone has come to imagining David's thoughts:

How Much Can Happen in Five Minutes?—Putting It All Together

1st minute—David gets off the bus and the neighbor's flag is in the wrong position. Again. He inhibits his compulsion to move it and reminds himself, "It's okay." His thoughts focus on the fact that all flags should be positioned with the pole on the left and the cloth on the right. David wants to rearrange the flag but decides it can wait for later when no one can tell him not to touch it. He lets out nervous laughter and shakes his hands up and down. He just noticed a strange car in his driveway that shouldn't be there. David's bus driver recognizes that he's getting stuck and gives him a reminder: "Come on, David. Let's go inside." David repeats, "Go inside now" and says, "work is done." He takes a final glance at the car and flag and begins to walk toward the door.

2nd minute—David makes it to his front door and the bus driver says, "Have a nice day." David's on his third week of a bipolar low and every day has been hard. He doesn't feel anything nice inside at all. He enters his house and doesn't hear the doorbell ring as it usually does and he wonders why. He makes sure everything else in his house is in order. He goes to his room and it looks right; he goes into the bathroom and puts the toilet lid down and washes his hands. Two times. He goes into his housemate's room, and that person screams, "Get out of here, David, or I'm going to hit you!" David repeats loudly, "Get out, David. I'm going to hit you." He's starting to feel a lot of stress and storms into the kitchen to look for staff.

3rd minute—When David walks into his kitchen, he sees the new staff member sitting at the table. She ignores his presence. The table that's supposed to be clean for dinner has a lot of paper on it. This new person reads the local newspaper instead of guidelines to help her interact with David. She thinks David's just an out-of-control person who needs to be treated like a child. She wonders what he's going to do next.

4th minute—David knows there shouldn't be anything on that table unless it's food. This stranger shouldn't have taken the place of the familiar person, the paper shouldn't be in that spot, and the one he expected to be making him dinner isn't here. He remembers he was chased around at work all day by some other staff person telling him to stop putting his hands in the trash. David knows if he touches those papers now, the new person may get upset, but his compulsion is building. That flag outside is still out of position, the car shouldn't be in his driveway, the doorbell's not ringing, the person who fixes dinner should be here by now, the trash at work still needs to be compacted, his housemate said, "I'm going to hit you," the papers on the table should be recycled, this stranger shouldn't be here . . .

5th minute—David walks up and grabs the newspaper the staff member is reading. She has a shocked expression on her face and tries to pull the paper back. She doesn't know how to work with this resident. David yanks the newspaper out of her hand and puts it where it belongs. He asks her if the person who's supposed to be cooking dinner is coming. She tells him to sit down and a housemate repeats the order, adding "You stupid idiot!" David reassures himself "It's okay" and sits in his chair scanning the environment to make sure everything else is in place. His mind is racing. He wants to pace, but he knows he's supposed to sit down. He runs out of his house, walks into his neighbor's yard and adjusts the flag.

This scenario reveals several typical autistic behaviors: the need for sameness (The neighbor's flag must face the same direction, strange cars shouldn't park in the driveway, the doorbell must ring, the toilet lid must remain down, housemates must leave their rooms in a particular condition, and the dining table must be cleared.); the repetition of other people's words ("Go inside now" and "Get out, David. I'm going to hit you."); repetitive movements (hand flapping and pacing); and ritualistic behaviors (the need for a rigid inspection of the house after being away). It also shows obsessive-compulsive disorder (repetitive hand washing and compacting trash).

I looked back wistfully to the time when David's major problem seemed to be his phobia about dogs. Now, his childish fears are replaced by adult ones. The triggering forces are less tangible, impossible for him or anyone else to grasp and express. Most of us accept that the things in our world are impermanent. David can't do this. In his twenties, when I threw the wilted daisies into the garbage, he pulled them out and assured me they would be all right if they drank more water. When the trees fell, he begged the wind to stop and insisted workmen not cut the trees for firewood. When someone ripped the page off the wall calendar at work, he tried frantically to tape the page back to the wall. Each time order was broken, he tried to restore it. Now, at thirty-nine, he must try to reassemble pieces of himself.

30

Christmas Eve Meltdown
David's Demons . . . My Demons

Phil picked David up at the group home and took him out to lunch while my mother and I peeled potatoes and threw together a Waldorf salad. I ironed white napkins embroidered with holly and aligned each knife, fork, and spoon on the dining room table. Mother was putting finishing touches on the centerpiece when David opened the front door and peered warily inside.

He'd visited his grandmother every Christmas Eve since his birth except the one after my father died, when we held our Christmas party in a motel room at the coast because we couldn't bear to be at my parents' home. Even then, David had been part of our celebration. Now he appeared afraid to enter his grandmother's apartment, though he'd been there many times.

"Hi, David, how are you?" My mother spoke in her usual cheerful tone but with an extra measure of kindness. David was her first grandchild, and they'd been close when he was young. I'd told her about his increased anxiety over the past few months.

"How was lunch?" I asked. Since David didn't answer, I tried again: "Did Dad take you to Burger King?" Usually, David felt obligated to give a short answer: "Lunch was good. Yeah, went to Burger King." This time he walked toward the coat closet, talking to himself: "No work, no work." As he hung up his jacket, his hands trembled.

I wasn't surprised he didn't say hello to his grandmother or me, but he didn't stop talking when we spoke to him. His thoughts seemed stuck in an endless loop. No messages could get through to him.

David went into the bathroom at the back of the apartment, probably to perfect the alignment of the towels on the rack and to give each a squeeze. He came back into the living room booming, "No work? . . . Go to the beach? . . . Who will cook dinner at the group home?" He asked each question as though his life depended on the answer. At first, my mom and I replied, "You don't have to work, David. It's a holiday . . . You're spending the night here with us, remember? You can go to the beach in January . . . We don't know who's cooking dinner at the group home, but we're cooking dinner here." When we could see he wasn't listening, we gave up. He wasn't looking for answers; he was trying to shed his anxiety.

I felt sorry we wouldn't take David to our house after Christmas, but he couldn't enjoy the beach. He couldn't enjoy anything. I looked at him as he paced the house. His hair wasn't washed, and he needed a haircut and shave. He wore an old pair of jeans with a red polo shirt. Though the shirt's color was appropriate, it was too small and its short sleeves didn't suit the weather. We'd given David two long-sleeved, easy-care shirts and a navy sweater as an early Christmas gift. I realized now I'd wanted to make him look good to offset his difficult behavior. I hoped he would wear his new plaid shirt for this gathering, but I wasn't surprised he wore something else. His aversion to new things intensified with anxiety.

My sister and her husband, my brother and his wife, another brother, and our son Jon and daughter, Lisa, arrived. A few friends came, too. One by one they spoke to David, attempting to make a connection. No one could penetrate his compulsive walking, talking, eating, and drinking. I felt sorry for them and for David, too.

My mother's apartment was laid out with the living, dining, and family areas in a semi-circle around a small central kitchen. Two bedrooms at the back of the house flanked a small bathroom. David walked rapidly from room to room, a difficult feat with so many bodies in the way. Each time he passed through the semi-circle, like a planet in its orbit, he snagged a handful of Chex Party Mix from the buffet and another glass of soda, juice, or water from the kitchen.

As he walked, he almost grazed each person he passed. The person moved out of his way and went on talking as though nothing happened. I gave my family high marks for sensitivity, but I felt defeated. David's ability to move among us, yet remain outside the family fabric, symbolized all that had gone wrong the past three years. He was physically with us but mentally and emotionally absent. Autism's worst aspects, its social isolation and fixed behaviors, had been magnified by his anxiety and obsessions. Even going somewhere he liked was stressful. He didn't trust people the way he had as a child and a young adult; he looked constantly on edge.

Phil took David for a walk, trying to calm him, but he returned as agitated as before. My mother dragged old photo albums from the top shelf of her coat closet and sat next to him on her flowered sofa. She pointed to the people in his life he seemed to have forgotten. David looked intently at the pictures, his eyes riveted on photos of himself as a young person with grandparents and with extended family at birthday celebrations and holidays. This was the first time he'd been quiet since he arrived.

Maybe he's trying to recapture parts of himself, I thought. He looked peaceful, gazing at the pictures. Apparently, a connection with people was easier when they were flat figures on a page. After five minutes, though, he set the album aside and walked over to the Chex Mix.

"I like you," he said to his grandmother between fits of restlessness. She asked me later, "What did he mean when he said that?"

"I think those are words he wants to hear from you," I told her. "He wants your reassurance that you still like him because his housemates yell at him to be quiet and stop messing with their things. He doesn't think anyone likes him anymore."

We planned to eat dinner, attend a candlelight church service, and come back to the apartment for cookies and coffee or hot chocolate. Instead, Phil stayed home with David during the service. His loud talking would have been disruptive, and we didn't think he'd enjoy the event as he had in the past.

When I returned after church, David still paced and talked loudly. Phil had given him his meds at 7:00, an hour earlier than usual but within the allowed window. Although David should have been sedated from a large dose of Seroquel, he was still super-charged. Had there been caffeine in his pop? Had he consumed too much sugar? Why didn't his medication calm him?

I piled Spritz, Chocolate Crinkles, and Mexican Wedding Cakes on a plate. I wondered how David could eat anything more, but he shoveled in cookies and gulped hot chocolate without any sign of enjoyment.

A neighbor dropped by and we visited until almost 11:00. After the guest left, I asked David to get into his pajamas while Phil and I put linens on his hide-a-bed, located in the living room. We made the bed and Phil went into another area to watch T.V.

As my mom and I sat in the living room, David came out of the bathroom carrying his dirty clothes in one hand and holding a pair of plaid pajama bottoms around his waist with the other. The pajama pants seemed cut for someone short and fat, not tall and thin.

They must have belonged to one of David's housemates.

When David bent over to put his underwear into his duffel bag, he let go of the pajama bottoms. They fell to the floor. With his pants around his feet, he slowly smoothed his clothes inside the bag as if nothing had happened.

I glanced at my mother to see her reaction. She seemed to be taking the appearance of her adult grandson in the buff only six feet from us with aplomb.

Though others might have seen humor in the situation, I didn't. I would have been embarrassed for my mother to see David naked anyway, but I felt especially chagrined because of the size of his testicles. He'd been tested twice for Fragile X Syndrome, a genetic condition involving changes in the X chromosome which causes enlarged testicles. It's the most common form of inherited intellectual disability in boys and can be a cause of autism.[14]

When David was eighteen, three doctors at Oregon Health and Science University said they were 90% certain he had the disorder because of his autism, large ears, and enlarged testicles. The results of the blood test came back negative, however. A more sophisticated genetic test a few years later was negative, too. Since there was no treatment for the disorder, I dismissed the subject.

"Pull your pants up, David!" I screamed. I tried to help him secure the waist, but the pants continued to fall off as he walked around the room. Since he wouldn't stop walking, I finally ordered, "Go to bed!" If he covered himself with sheets and a blanket, my mother and I wouldn't have to see his private parts.

Instead of getting into the hide-a-bed, David became agitated. I'd made a huge mistake: In my haste to see him clothed, I'd given him two commands. He couldn't stand to be reprimanded.

Shaking, David dug his red polo shirt out of his duffel bag and went into the guest bedroom. When I entered the room, he stood next to the bed wiping the wall with his red polo shirt, his pajama bottoms again at his feet. "No work! No work! No work!" The muscles in his face twitched. He breathed rapidly.

"David, stop!" I grabbed his arm. His skin felt wet with sweat. He kept wiping.

I lowered my voice: "David, stop." He went on wiping. He didn't seem to know I was in the room.

Later, I remembered an incident report from his work program the year before which said he'd taken off his shirt in the bathroom and wiped the walls. Had this action become a ritual? What did it mean?

Phil came into the bedroom and maneuvered David back into the living room. In a few minutes, he slid under the covers of the hide-a-bed. After we turned off the light, he quieted down but continued to talk to himself. Mother went to her room, and I brushed my teeth and got into bed.

By 12:30, I couldn't hear David talking anymore. I lay next to Phil, my heart pounding. What was David thinking when he wiped his shirt on the wall? Why wouldn't—or couldn't—he stop? *He's completely disintegrated,* I thought. *My child's gone and in his place is this wild man who disrupts family gatherings and destroys our hopes for him.* Up until this time, David's difficult behaviors had been mostly relegated to his workplace, day program, or group home. Now they were on full display for our family, relatives, and friends—those who had known David from birth and loved him. My grief felt overwhelming.

"He's turned into a monster," I wailed to my mother in the kitchen the next morning, after little sleep.

"It was confusing for him with so many people here." She was filling the coffee maker with water, so I couldn't see her face, but she sounded tired.

I felt remorse for upsetting her. My reactions to David's behavior hadn't helped the situation. I could usually remain calm, but this time my fears and my pride had gotten the best of me. Why had I called David a monster? Hadn't I advocated for years to keep others from thinking this way? Yes, his actions were bizarre, but if his family couldn't show understanding, who could?

My angst continued after Phil and I returned home. In my journal, I dubbed David's Christmas Eve meltdown "the mad scene." For the first time since his diagnosis of a developmental delay at two-and-a-half years, I felt wronged as a parent. David seemed to have passed the point where I could connect with him. Why wouldn't . . . why couldn't . . . he listen to me? When he was twenty-five, he'd paced and talked loudly at Christmas, but his behavior hadn't been completely out of control. After the holiday, he'd asked me, "Don't worry about Christmas Day?" as if he wanted reassurance the world would go on in spite of his behavior. Now, I didn't have the consolation of talking to him about his actions.

By the end of January, I was able to put the events of Christmas Eve in better perspective. I'd written in my journal that David trampled others' thoughts and dreams. Now, I realized that under his feet lay his own trampled dreams. When he said, "No work, no work," he wasn't saying "I don't want to work." He was saying, "Work isn't possible for me anymore. I can't stay at my work table; I have to get up and walk. I can't hold the bag to put things inside because my hands shake too much. I'm thirsty all the time. When I get more juice or pop, people yell at me. They shout at me when I straighten papers or push down the trash to make it neater. I can't do anything right, and nobody wants me around."

Like everyone, David felt the assault of things he couldn't control and the flux of his own emotions, but autism gave him fewer defenses against that assault. He also didn't understand how hard his doctor, case advocates, vocational and residential managers, behavioral specialists, and family were looking for answers. He didn't know we'd tried desperately to get him into an Alternative-to-Employment program where he wouldn't have to work, but every effort had failed.

He felt alone. He couldn't hold his own against the chaos in the world and in his own head.

If only he could wipe out this chaos by rubbing his shirt against a wall.

31

Growing into a Family
Acceptance and Respect

Nine months after David's Christmas Eve meltdown, Phil and I made a five-day trip to Sunriver with two of our three adult children—David, still at the height of his anxiety and obsessive-compulsive disorder, and Lisa, eight years younger, upset by her brother's behavior in the past. Our son Jon stayed behind to work in Portland. It had been several years since the four of us had spent this much time together. I wanted things to go well for each of us and for family unity, but this vacation had the earmarks of a disaster.

An unexpected rain had fallen since we left Portland. David and I sat in the back seat of our blue Subaru as we hurtled along the Santiam River. Phil drove and Lisa sat in the front passenger seat, her blond ponytail pressed against the headrest. I'd offered her this position so she could gaze at the whitewater and mossy rocks of the meandering river and visit with her dad.

The novel in my lap was about a group of people who lived together as a family out of necessity and mutual consent—people who weren't related. Would such a family be easier or harder to form than one connected by blood? Creating any kind of family required grit, I decided.

"Goody's, go, Trout House Restaurant, go." David chanted the names of an ice cream shop and a restaurant in Sunriver. We'd go there, I assured him, my responses on autopilot. I wondered again why he placed the verb last in his litanies but didn't do this in ordinary speech.

"How're ya doin,' David?" He channeled a staff member at his workplace, taking his own emotional temperature. *Not very well,* I thought. He seemed to be asking himself, "Am I okay? Am I safe? Do I like going on vacation?" He'd never been good at assessing his own feelings, and our reassurances no longer comforted him. Increased anxiety meant more voices jostling for attention in his head.

He wrinkled his nose. A long "A-a-a-a-a-a" emanated from his throat. Could things possibly get any worse?

"The creaking door," I said and jotted down the new sound for his psychiatrist. David looked at my notepad with suspicion. I felt guilty. Was he becoming only a case to be analyzed?

"Kermit the Frog," Phil offered. "David, are you Kermit?"

Lisa frowned at her father.

Looking out the window, David didn't answer. In most families, our banter wouldn't have meant anything, but I was afraid we'd teased him unfairly. He probably hadn't been aware of the sound he made, and he didn't understand teasing because he couldn't determine others' motives. Since he seemed to be in his own world, it had been easy to talk about him as if he weren't there or as if he didn't have feelings. Family dynamics were tough when the players weren't on even ground.

We arrived in Sunriver and turned on the heat. A thermometer outside the patio door read 55 degrees, cool for early September in Central Oregon.

The rain continued for two days. David paced the house and squeezed the bath towels in both bathrooms like the man in the old Charmin commercial squeezed a toilet paper roll. As he compressed the towels, he talked to himself. I hoped the skies would clear long enough for him to walk and for Lisa to take pictures.

Stir-crazy, we drove to the outlet stores in Bend. Phil and David waited in the car while Lisa bought gift wrap and I picked out fall napkins and a Casper-like ghost for David to hang in his home. He usually liked holiday decorations, but when I showed him this one, he said without enthusiasm, "Yeah, it's a ghost."

That evening, Lisa and I made meat loaf and garlic mashed potatoes for supper. Phil watched the news, and David wandered back and forth through the kitchen, talking loudly: "Group home, go. Group home, go . . ." He probably dreaded returning home because he'd be in trouble for reorganizing objects in his housemates' rooms and in the staff office and for talking loudly.

When he first moved to the group home, he'd looked forward to returning there after visits with us. Now he didn't feel comfortable anywhere, not even on vacation.

Lisa and I shared sympathetic looks. She put garlic in the press. "We can move away from David's anxiety, but he can't." I hadn't thought of it this way. He was caught in the eye of the hurricane; we were removed most of the time. I was impressed by her empathy. She was taking a larger role in David's life, attending his Individual Support Plan meetings and helping to plan for his future. At thirty-one, she had a job at a graphics company, but the work was mundane and she wasn't using her art degree. Though her own life seemed on hold, she related more to David than ever before.

She dumped crushed garlic into the pan of red potatoes. "Maybe if David's doctor can get the medications right, he'll be able to carry on a conversation again. It's hard to feel close to him now." I nodded. She added more garlic. "I felt a little connection with him when he was in high school learning job skills. But now so much of his communication is telling us what he doesn't want."

I took the meat loaf out of the oven, remembering how David said, "No work, no work" every time he talked to Phil or me on the phone, as if pleading with us to allow him to stay home. He wasn't happy at work or at home, and we didn't know what to do.

Lisa looked in the drawer for the potato masher. "There was a glimmer of hope for me when he said he'd like to have copies of the pictures I took of him. He was able to express something he wanted."

Three months before, she'd taken a photo of David sitting on a log at the beach, his fingers laced in his lap. It had been hard to find a time when he wasn't twitching his nose, frowning, and working his jaw. Somehow, Lisa managed to catch him in a natural pose, almost calm, almost his old self. I'd shown him the picture and asked if he wanted a copy. He said yes.

The photo reminded me of a picture Lisa drew of David from a photograph. Four years old, he sits on a sandbank, wearing a rain slicker with the sleeves rolled up. His hands are crossed in a pensive pose. He looks down at his shiny new rain boots. One boot lies straight ahead; the other's twisted to one side. A shadow across his face emphasizes his repose. He's half-smiling: a small boy alone, at peace with his surroundings.

An image is superimposed in the upper left corner of the drawing: A huge, light-bejeweled starfish rests in a sparkling tide pool, three arms wrapped around a barnacled rock. The oversized sea creature makes the boy appear smaller, but he looks safe, locked in his reverie. The juxtaposition of images captures an important aspect of David's childhood: Though he was in many ways closed off from others, he was free of worry. If only he could regain this sense of peace.

Lisa attacked the red potatoes with a masher. "I wish his life could feel rewarding to him again."

We filled the plates with comforting food, sad we couldn't change things.

By Friday, the skies cleared. Lisa took out her camera and tripod, and Phil guided her to nooks along the Deschutes River. I drove with her to take pictures of Lava Butte. After he walked the bike trails, David seemed calmer, closer to the person Lisa captured in her drawing of him as a child.

Our family has grown closer as the children have become adults. Jon and Lisa realize David needs their understanding and support. After the trip to Sunriver with David and Lisa, I asked Jon what he thought about his brother's difficult behaviors. He said, "David does things the way he needs to do them so he can keep going." If David had been able to talk about Jon, he might have said the same thing.

Phil and I have understood each other better in retirement, without the distractions of daily employment. We've worked together to ensure David has the best chance for success, and Jon and Lisa have our love and support. Looking back, I've asked myself what allowed Phil and me to stay together despite the demands of raising David and two other children with their own unique needs. I would like to say love held us together, but I think it's more truthful to say our strong commitment to each other and our family didn't allow us to consider leaving.

When Phil and I married, I admired his dependability. Over the years, I've often wished he would surprise me with tickets to a play or concert, a quick hug, or a smile. These actions are not in his nature. He likes to plan even the smallest activity:

working in the yard or taking a walk. Sometimes, I look for excitement in our relationship, forgetting it was Phil's dependability that attracted me to him in the first place.

Though Phil's interests tend toward building and finance, he supports my love of books and writing, often doing household chores so I can write. In our first two homes, he built a desk for me in our bedroom and stained bookcases for the living room. In our present home, he carved out a study for me and indulged my wish for a library. He once noted Thomas Jefferson had a reading station with four sides so he could read four books at one time. Phil was interested in how the station was built, while I marveled that Jefferson read four books at one time.

It's 5 a.m. Our bedroom window is open, and I can hear the ocean two blocks away. A warm blanket is pulled over my shoulders and around my neck. Phil covers me when it's cold, as he tucked our children into their beds when they were young. Covering me with a blanket is his way of making sure I'm safe and warm. When the children were sick or hurt, we both rushed to help them, but it was Phil who sat with them for hours to soothe them.

I snuggle into the covers and fall back asleep. In personal relationships—the long, important ones—what we value most is often hidden.

32

The Calming Room
Behavioral Intervention

After Phil and I had almost given up on finding a
behavior specialist with experience in autism in the
Portland area, we found Marie Johnson. Two months
later, Marie and I sat in her small upstairs office talking
about David's progress at Empowerment Services, a
behavioral program for autistic children and adults she
ran in her home. Suddenly David's loud voice erupted
from the "classroom" down the hall. I couldn't make
out his words, but something had triggered a protest.

"Do you want to come and watch?" Marie
motioned me to follow her. We walked toward a tiny
bedroom called the calming room. David and Victoria,
the young, blond assistant who'd been working with
him in the classroom, were already there. David sat at a
small table, Victoria on his right. I took a seat behind
David, close enough to see what was happening.

Marie flipped off the lights and pulled up a chair
in front of David. He put his head down on the small
table. Apparently, he knew the drill. Marie whispered,
"When you can use your quiet voice, we're going to

count to ten." Her tone was supportive, as though she was on his side.

He started to count: "One, two, three, four . . ." His voice rose quickly, building toward another rant.

"Oh, we're going to start over." Marie was matter-of-fact, speaking almost in a whisper. David put his head down.

I was struck by the incongruity of this scene. David wasn't a three-year-old learning to control temper tantrums; he was a forty-year-old, 6 foot 3-inch man with almost no understanding of his own emotions, trying to learn to control them.

When he'd finished counting to ten without raising his voice, Marie put a plastic bin of tiny colored blocks on the table. "Victoria's going to sort with you." Victoria began sorting and then turned the task over to David.

"One yellow, one blue . . . one yellow, one blue." His fingers fumbled with the blocks. He could have performed this exercise correctly when he was eight, but anxiety prevented him from doing it now. I felt sick, thinking how much ground he'd lost.

"Group home go, Burger King go . . ." He was beginning another rant.

"Oh, now we're going to do a calmer again." Marie's voice didn't show a hint of exasperation, as mine would have.

"One yellow, one blue . . ." This time David sorted the blocks in the bowl correctly.

Marie praised him. "I'm going to give you a point. You're talking very quietly. You're staying in your chair. I like that."

Victoria put the blocks away, took a bin of beans from the shelf, and began to count. "One brown, two brown, three, four, five. Five browns. One black, two black, three, four, five. Five black beans. Do you want to count to five or ten?" Always give a choice—I remembered this advice given when David was a toddler.

"Ten," David said, counting the beans correctly.

Marie stepped in again. "Nice job. You stopped, looked, and listened, and then you did it the right way." Positive reinforcement. I could see David relaxing. He would have remembered these words from his eighteen years in special ed. He probably felt relieved to go back to a system he knew after the negative feedback of staff, housemates, and coworkers.

"Are you feeling calmer?" Marie looked at him.

"Yeah."

"I'll show you on your calendar." She placed her index finger low on a thermometer image on the page. "Are you ready to check your schedule?"

"Yeah."

David followed Victoria back to the classroom, his head bent in a familiar pose. He was learning to calm himself. His visual schedule, a series of pictures telling him what he would do that day, provided a needed structure. Marie's method was working.

We had known since David was young he needed a high degree of structure. He was happy as a schoolchild with a consistent schedule; he floundered as an adult production worker with changes in daily routine. In an attempt to provide a supportive framework now, Marie devised a visual system called a life binder, tailored to David's needs. This binder consisted of the following sections:

> *Emotions*—Faces represent different feelings such as calm, angry, or sad. David points to the picture that best expresses how he feels.

> *Thermometer*—A thermometer graphic has a scale from 1 to 10 (1 being "in bed" and 10 being in a crisis state of anxiety). David attaches the picture closest to his emotion to the Velcro strip on the point of the scale that matches his anxiety level.

> *Calmers*—Pictures suggest things David can do to calm down if he's upset, such as listen to music, put his head down, or go for a walk. He needs to know he has choices.

> *Self-control strip*—He attaches appropriate pictures from his calmers to help him use self-control if he's stressed or anxious.

Daily schedule—A visual schedule helps him transition from one activity to the next. It creates structure and predictability, which reduce anxiety.

Problem solving—Pictures help him figure out what the problem is and how to solve it. For example, if he feels sick, he can point to the appropriate icon and look for a picture that shows what he should do.

Social Stories—These are tools for teaching social skills to people with autism and related disabilities. For example, a friend wrote a social story for David to help him overcome his fear of dogs.

Not only did David need structure in his activities, but he needed consistent, kind direction. In her book, *Autism: A Very Short Introduction,* Uta Frith writes, the best school environment for a child with autism is a "calming environment and a highly structured and firm teaching style, tempered by kindness."[15] I think the same qualities provide the best living and working environment for adults.

After David attended Marie's school for four months, we helped him move from his work program to an ATE (Alternative-to-Employment) program run by his residential provider. There, he used the calmers Marie developed as he put together puzzles, went on walks, visited the library, and performed simple janitorial tasks. Although the move from his work program was stressful, he found friends among the new staff. He had more trouble winning over the other clients, who had difficulty understanding his loud talk and compulsive behaviors.

In the group home, old habits had become ingrained and more difficult to change, and David did not have one-on-one staff, as he had at the ATE program. A behavior specialist employed by David's residential provider consulted with Marie Johnson to develop a behavior plan for him, but implementation was slow. She tried to set up a calming area in David's bedroom similar to the one at Marie's house, but David didn't want his room to change.

Efforts to train residential staff in how to use his life binder didn't work, either. The new behavior specialist videotaped the one-on-one staff member at David's day program using his binder with him, but she had trouble with the tape and I never heard if it was used to train the group home staff. She developed a tracking form for staff to make reports to the psychiatrist and ISP team more objective, but that, too, seemed futile.

Marie's goal had been to teach David to be calm in all environments by using his life binder. This did not work in the group home. Staff reported he was running around the house and bouncing on his bed. Even when he went into the community, he seemed frantic. He was banned from using his TriMet lift bus six times in one month for unbuckling his seat belt while the bus was running. He told himself, "You're a good guy; you know better, David," but his challenging behaviors continued. I could only imagine how difficult things must have been for the staff and other residents at 89th Court.

The situation was wrenching for David, too. He lived with housemates he couldn't understand and who couldn't understand him. As he stormed through the house, he looked gaunt from weight loss. He seemed in constant motion. We've heard of restless leg syndrome; what would it be like to have restless body syndrome? For the previous three years, David's psychiatrist had searched without success for a medication—or combination of medications—to alleviate his anxiety. Some tranquilizers and mood stabilizers only seemed to increase his agitation.

I didn't know the answers, but David needed to be comfortable with his environment in order to be comfortable with himself. Maybe Phil and I should help him move to a different home, but we worried that even if the mix of residents and staff were favorable when David moved in, circumstances could change. And the move itself would cause anxiety. We didn't know what to do.

33

The End Waves at You from the Beginning
The Move from 89th Court

When David moved to a group home at age thirty, our family considered his future secure. He had an easy relationship with housemates and staff and a packaging job he enjoyed.

His first eight years at 89th Court were mostly happy. But from late 2008 to 2012, the makeup of clients and staff changed. David became distraught and disruptive in his home and at his worksite.

Phil and I attended meeting after meeting, received second opinions on his meds, and consulted with behavior specialists but saw no improvement in David's mood and behavior.

The only option left was to help him move to a different home. But this appeared risky given his reactions to change in the past. His services coordinator warned the move might "push him over the edge." And even a home that seemed ideal at first could fluctuate. We didn't know if change would lead to a better life for David. Our fear of the unknown stymied us.

At 5:30, I turned on the evening news and waited for Phil to join me. The phone rang. Phil answered in the kitchen and called me to get on a second phone—never a good sign. This must be about one of the kids, I thought as I picked up the receiver.

"Roy Soards here." Roy was the northwest director for Bethesda Lutheran Communities, David's residential and day program provider. He'd never called before, though I knew him from family association meetings and a visit to our house two years before to help us problem-solve David's behavior issues. Roy gave us the name of Marie Johnson, the behavior specialist who taught David calming strategies and a visual system to communicate his feelings.

Roy struggled to keep his managerial tone. I could tell this was a call he didn't want to make. His voice seemed far away. Finally, meaning began to form in my mind: It had been a hard decision, but Bethesda could no longer serve David. His loud talk and racing through rooms made his housemates fearful in their own home. Roy was sorry, but a change in environment might be better for David, too.

"There really should be more services for folks like David," he continued. What folks, I wondered—those with mental health issues on top of developmental disabilities? I didn't want David lumped in with faceless others. How many of these *folks* had been asked to leave their homes? I'd only heard of two in all the years I'd worked with other family members in our support organization. Maybe this was something people didn't talk about, like a child being called to the principal's office.

I wanted to scream or at least defend our position. The manager and lead staff at David's home reassured us only three weeks earlier that the situation was manageable. Roy had vowed two years before he would never ask David to leave his home.

"How much time do we have to find a new place?" Phil asked. Always practical, he knew this would be a challenge. What if we only had a month? My heart beat in my throat.

Roy hoped we could find a place in sixty days. Of course, Bethesda wouldn't throw David out. They'd serve him until we could find a good placement. Roy's reassurances did little to calm my fears. What if there wasn't a place? What if no one wanted David?

I thought of something else: "What about his day program? Can he keep that?" It had only been a year-and-a-half since we'd helped David move from his work program to an Alternative-to-Employment program. Things were going fairly well there, though David needed one-on-one staff most of the time, and his service payment didn't allow for this level of care. Money was always a factor with any placement. The service payment had to be adequate to cover staffing.

Roy was sorry. Bethesda couldn't provide services for David at the day program, either. He wished things were different. Phil and I thanked him and hung up.

With one phone call, David's future had evaporated. A former writing teacher once commented, "The end waves at you from the beginning." The end had been waving at us for at least two years, but we'd chosen not to see it.

Setting aside national news in favor of our own, Phil and I discussed exploring adult foster care, a program in which a licensed person provides twenty-four-hour care to seniors or adults with physical or intellectual disabilities in a single-family residence. The care provider must complete a basic training course and pass an exam to be licensed.

We had visited an adult foster home a few months earlier on the recommendation of a fellow church member whose brother lived there. She said the provider's gentle, yet firm approach worked miracles with her brother. We knew some adult foster homes had only two or three residents, as opposed to five in group homes. The fewer housemates the better, we reasoned, since David's loud talk and pacing wore thin on those around him, and he felt calmer in a quiet environment.

We also hoped fewer staff and a live-in provider would offer more consistency in care. David often worried when a staff member didn't show up for his shift or the staff schedule changed. It would be good to minimize these problems.

When we finished talking, Phil called David's case manager and left a voicemail asking him to initiate the process of assessment for adult foster care. We would have to move quickly to find a new home for

David in only two months. We could change our minds later if we decided this wasn't the right course.

The next day, I couldn't stop thinking about Roy's call. I knew he cared about Bethesda's clients and their families. And though the program manager and lead staff at David's home reassured us that David's behaviors were manageable, tensions had escalated. When we called the home, we often heard David shouting in the background. Sometimes he was so agitated he wouldn't come to the phone.

Yet, 89th Court was David's home. How could we move him without his consent, or even his understanding of why this was happening? We couldn't sit down with him to talk about his situation. We had to make a decision for him.

Eleven years before, we'd received an unexpected phone call to notify us that a group home placement was available. That call had brought hope. Roy's call confirmed how far David had slipped in the previous three years and intensified our disappointment that we hadn't been able to stop his slide.

We received official written notification of Roy's decision from Bethesda's area director two days later: "Please consider this email the formal request to exit your son, David Mannan, from residential and vocational services with Bethesda Lutheran Communities." The director reiterated this had been a difficult decision, but the organization thought David would be better served in an environment more suited to his needs. There was no mention of the group home staff's inability, or unwillingness, to implement David's behavior plan, no "We regret that we can no longer provide residential services for your son. We've enjoyed serving David, and we will miss him." The words "exit your son" made him an object to be dealt with, rather than a respected client and a beloved son. If Roy had not called us earlier to soften the blow, I would have been furious.

Yet, David hadn't been happy at 89th Court for the past three years. The situation had become untenable, and he needed to move for his own wellbeing. Roy's phone call and the area director's notification simply forced our hand.

The next morning, I thanked the area director for notifying us that we needed to help David move and for Bethesda's efforts on his behalf. In spite of the wording in her exit letter—perhaps dictated by national headquarters—David's group home manager, case manager-advocate, and behavior specialist had spent many hours over the previous three years trying to help him.

I thanked the residents and staff at 89th Court, too. They had been David's family, and therefore our family. Since David couldn't express his appreciation, I did it for him. The only resident who'd been in the home when David moved there was Joe, now in his eighties. Though nonverbal, he spoke through his smile as he flipped through the pages of his favorite magazines. I was sorry David had often carted away his magazines to straighten the living room. I hoped Joe forgave him. I hoped all the residents forgave him for interfering with their prized possessions.

Of the current staff, I would especially miss Nyamu, who'd said of David's trial sleepover eleven years before, "It was not impossible." He was the only staff member who remained from that time. He'd shown enormous patience during David's three-year downslide. "David has changed so much," Nyamu lamented, shaking his head as I dropped David off after a visit.

Soon after David was asked to leave his home, 89th Court's program manager emailed us a report, "Unusual Incident Report: Regarding the milk being poured out." This is the incident as I reconstructed it from her report:

David took an unopened gallon of milk from the refrigerator, poured himself a glass, and dumped the rest of the milk from the jug into the sink. Ivan (not the person's real name), one of two staff members on duty at the home that morning, said, "David what are you doing?" Ignoring the question, David took another gallon of milk from the fridge, drank a glass, and emptied the rest down the drain. He rinsed the two plastic jugs and took them to the recycling bin in the garage. Then he sat in a chair in the living room, shaking.

In answer to the question, "What was the person/ staff/others doing before the incident occurred?" the manager wrote, *David was yelling and running.* She offered no reason. Under "Injury," she checked *No.* She characterized David's actions as *Not respecting property.* Though the report raised several questions, I applauded her response to the incident: She advised staff to take David for a walk to buy some milk.

We had no way of knowing what led up to the incident or what was going through David's mind when he dumped two almost-full gallons of milk into the sink. The only clue lay with the staff person who filed the report. David had never gotten along well with Ivan. David preferred staff suggest what he should do; Ivan had a habit of giving orders. David wanted people to speak softly; Ivan spoke loudly. Since David can't judge how others feel by their words or body language, he uses tone of voice as a gauge. Whatever the reasons, the relationship between David and Ivan had always been contentious.

In the larger scheme of things, David pouring out two gallons of milk seemed minor. Yes, it was inconvenient for staff to make a special trip to the store. Yes, the action was wasteful, and David shouldn't have done it. But what was behind his behavior . . . a struggle for control?

I flipped to page four of the report. Next to "Did staff follow the Behavior Support Plan?" the program manager had written, *No.* In another place she noted, *No Behavioral Communication Involved.* By the time of the incident, the strain between David and staff may have been too great to successfully use behavioral measures. But the question remains, why had staff *never* used his Behavior Support Plan? Why hadn't they pointed to the pictures in his life binder that represented feelings and asked, "Which picture shows how you're feeling?" Why hadn't they pulled out his picture of a thermometer with gradations to indicate anxiety level and said, "Point to how you feel?" Why hadn't they used pictures in the problem solving section of his binder or helped him write a social story about a frustrating situation?

David, I wish we could have heard your voice, your side of the story. You were happy in your home for the first eight years. What made you unhappy? Why were you shouting as you ran through the house? *What* were you shouting? Was pouring out the milk a final salvo: "I'm fed up with being told what to do and I don't care anymore what anyone says?"

All we have to go by is an incident report and two empty milk jugs.

As we dealt with David's day-to-day problems, Phil and I tried to assure ourselves we were making the right decision for his future. We checked the Oregon Adult Foster Home Administrative Rules (OARs) and found they were much the same as those for group homes. Foster homes had the same safeguards as group homes, and they, too, could have up to five residents. [16] David would not be guaranteed a smaller number of housemates, as we had hoped.

As Rich, David's county services coordinator, worked behind the scenes to schedule a new assessment of David's support needs, we worried sixty days would not be enough time to find a new home. We felt relieved when Rich called and said he had a date for the meeting.

The Support Needs Assessment Profile (SNAP) meeting was scheduled for July 20, 2012, sixteen days after Bethesda's request that David leave their programs—lightning speed for bringing together a residential program manager, vocational program manager, services coordinator, and guardians, as well as an assessor. This speed reflected the urgency of our task. Roy had given us sixty days to find new residential and vocational providers for David. Even with a grace period, this was a tight timeline.

The SNAP would determine David's service rate, the amount a provider would receive each month to provide for his care. It would list David's characteristics and say, "Can you serve this person?" It sounded like a cold assessment. As with all government-subsidized programs, adult foster care came down to dollars. An evaluation two years before had pegged David's needs at a level much lower than they actually were. I wondered whether this new assessment would serve him any better.

Strangely, David was not required to attend the meeting. Since we could complete the assessment without him, the team agreed he should attend his day program as usual. This made sense since he would have been upset to hear us discuss his behavior, he would not have been able to represent himself, and his loud repetitions would have made our deliberations difficult.

Still, I felt we were stripping him of his rights. My mind and my heart struggled to find a way to support his wishes, to know what they were. It seemed we were mates on a ship named David. We would hoist our sails and set off for an unknown destination while the one for whom we labored slept below deck.

I was even more upset when I found out a state Human Services Developmental Disabilities representative would determine David's level of care without meeting him or seeing him in a natural setting. The SNAP assessment would depend entirely upon what the five of us said about him. David had been termed "a protected person" in our guardianship document. He'd sometimes been called "an incapacitated person," as well. Was he now in danger of becoming a nonperson?

In the days leading up to the SNAP assessment, Phil and I lay awake at night, worrying about David's reaction to the upcoming changes. We remembered Rich's comment that a change of homes might push him over the edge. What would that mean—a crisis placement in which his condition would deteriorate even more? We also wondered whether it would be possible to find a provider, support staff, and housemates who were caring and accepting of David's loud talking and compulsive behaviors. If the assessment portrayed David as someone who ignored reasonable requests and ran roughshod over housemates, who would want to provide services for him?

"He's not like this," I wanted to shout. What about the first thirty-eight years of his life when family, teachers, group home staff, Special Olympics coaches, and recreation district day trip leaders all found him easy to redirect? He'd adopted unacceptable behaviors only after his life spun beyond his ability to cope, and he had no way to understand or express his anxiety.

After a night of tossing and turning, I emailed Rich to ask if we could submit written material showing David in a better light. He said no. But on the Department of Human Resources Needs Assessment website, under "Role of Respondents" (which I learned meant participants), I discovered we could bring a few pages of notes. I also found a fifty-eight-page document listing the questions the assessor would use at the meeting. I could prepare! Knowing what questions to expect and jotting down a few answers eased my mind.

Phil and I met with David's residential and vocational program managers and county services coordinator in the Washington County Public Services Building on July 20th. The mood in the room felt surprisingly relaxed. We discovered we knew the assessor's father, who had years before developed a visual plan for David when David worked at Tualatin Valley Workshop. Rich had been the program manager at TVW at that time. It seemed like old home week with these familiar faces.

For two hours, we answered questions about David's daily support needs at home, at work (or, in his case, an Alternative-to-Employment program), and in the community. Our considerations included the support he required for brushing his teeth, shaving, and other daily living activities, as well as communication, safety, medical care, and behavioral issues. The five of us agreed on almost every point. The sad truth was David now needed one-on-one staffing in almost every situation.

When we received the results of the SNAP assessment in the mail a few days later, we were amazed David's monthly service rate had been set at $6,492. This level of financial support should provide for his care if a licensed provider accepted him.

The next step was for Rich to send out a referral packet to adult foster care providers in the Portland area and surrounding region. The packet included the new assessment along with David's Individual Support Plan (ISP) and supporting documents, official papers related to his diagnosis and medical and behavioral issues, and a copy of our guardianship papers. The goal was to provide the information a potential provider required to decide whether he or she could meet David's support needs.

Within a week, Medhanie Embaye, in Saint Helens, Oregon, said he was interested in providing a home for David. Phil and I visited his home and decided it would be a suitable fit for David. Medhanie was soft-spoken and caring, the kind of caregiver David had liked in the past.

Though the home was in an industrial area with a school bus garage and recycling plant next-door, the rooms had fresh paint and new carpet, and they were clean.

The next week, Phil and I took David for a visit to Medhanie's home. David walked quickly to the front door.

"Ring the bell," I reminded him.

He pushed the bell, opened the door a crack, and peered into the living room. Medhanie, talking on his cell phone, motioned us inside.

David stood in the doorway, scanning the room. "No dogs?"

"No dogs," Medhanie reassured him, putting his cell phone in his pocket.

David sat gingerly on the plaid sofa near the front door, wearing his heavy winter jacket. He fixed his eyes on the big screen T.V. a few feet away. Medhanie had turned the channel to a program he thought David would like to watch. He'd made a good choice. David loved Barney, the purple dinosaur. For the rest of the visit, David sat with his eyes glued to the screen.

Though the visit went well, Phil and I wanted to wait to hear from other providers before making a decision that would affect David so greatly. Weeks went by. It seemed David was up for auction and no one was bidding. I checked with Rich every few days to see if he'd heard anything. Medhanie called each Friday to reaffirm his interest in serving David. I began to realize adult foster care was a business. Medhanie needed more income.

Finally, Rich called to say a representative from an organization headquartered in Warrenton, Oregon, an hour's drive from where we lived, wanted to visit David the next week. A provider in the Portland area who specialized in serving individuals with autism was also looking for another client and would visit David soon. This was good news, but we wished the opportunities had surfaced sooner. Not only was Medhanie eager to fill his vacancy, but we were approaching Roy Soards' sixty-day deadline to find new residential and vocational programs for David. As the deadline came and went, I emailed Roy an update and thanked him for his patience.

A week later, we still hadn't heard back from Rich about the visits from the two other providers who planned to visit David. I called Rich's office to find he was on vacation. I tracked down Josh, who'd done the SNAP assessment. Rich had told him what was happening before he left. The provider in the Portland area had decided against taking David. Josh agreed to call the other provider. In a few hours, he called back. The person was interested. Josh gave us the program manager's phone number. By that afternoon, we'd arranged a visit for the following Monday. Phil and I had high hopes for the home: It was in the country, only forty minutes from our house.

On a sunny fall day, we made the trip up the coast to Gearhart to meet the manager. He was afraid we'd never find the place on our own, so he asked us to meet him at a McDonald's in a nearby town and follow him in our car. At the end of a narrow lane, we came to a house with a worn roof and askew downspouts. A former ranch, the home consisted of a main house and several outbuildings. One of the outbuildings that looked barely habitable housed a client who was semi-independent.

In the main house, we met two staff and two residents: one in a wheelchair and the other using a walker. The residents didn't speak, so we couldn't learn their stories, but the staff seemed dispirited, and with stained toilets, holes in the walls, and some rooms stripped to the subfloor, why wouldn't they be dispirited? I felt sad for the residents in the home. How could they feel valued in these surroundings? Why had the state licensed such a home?

After the tour, the staff, manager, and county officials stood with us in a circle on a patio in the back yard. The staff and manager were optimistic about David's chances for success in their program. We talked about David's needs and said we'd get back to them. But I knew what our answer would be: There was no way we would ask David to live in a home we wouldn't live in ourselves, even if it were the only one available. We'd worked all his life to ensure he had the best opportunities possible. We wouldn't give up that effort now.

The next morning, I called Rich and asked him to set up an exit/entrance meeting for David to leave 89th

Court and move to Medhanie's home in Saint Helens, a formality required by the state.

After a moving date had been set, Phil and I laid out a plan to try to minimize the effect that leaving his home would have for David. We would meet Medhanie at 89th Court after David's bus picked him up for his day program in Hillsboro. The three of us would remove his possessions from his home and transport them to Saint Helens, about an hour away. At the new home, we would hang up David's clothes, set up his bed, dresser, and book case in his bedroom, and place his recliner in the living room. Then we would rush to Hillsboro, an hour's drive, to pick up David at his day program before staff left at 3:30.

We saw no way but to conduct the move without David. With his strong need for sameness and familiarity, it would have been wrenching for him to watch his possessions being hauled away. He would have tried to put things back where they belonged, as when he was a child and struggled to return Christmas ornaments to the tree as I removed them. As an adult, he had never allowed his bedroom furniture to be moved even two inches from its original position.

Though Phil and I agreed David should not take part in the move, we felt we were betraying his trust by moving him without his participation. I wished we could explain his position to him in a way he could grasp.

My feeling of betraying David was accompanied by sadness that he'd lost ground since he moved from our home. In the past three years, his anxiety made relating to others almost impossible. As a result, he now had an even smaller support system than before. As he'd dropped out of one activity after another, he'd become estranged from his few friends—if they could be called friends—from school, work, church, Special Olympics, and park district outings. His present contacts consisted of immediate family, relatives, staff and housemates at his home, and staff and clients at his day program. Now his world would shrink even more.

Because David had been asked to leave his home and day program, I felt he would not only leave without his understanding and approval, but he would leave in disgrace.

Phil and I arrived at 89th Court at 11:00 a.m., the arranged time. Medhanie and Nyamu stood exchanging stories on the sidewalk outside the house. Both had grown up in eastern Africa—Medhanie in Eritrea and Nyamu in Kenya. Both had given direct care to people with developmental disabilities in group homes in the Portland area. Recently, Medhanie had begun to provide foster care to people with the same kind of disabilities. Like many from other countries, Nyamu and Medhanie performed jobs many American-born people didn't want to do, for little more than minimum wage.

As Phil and I greeted the two men, David opened the front door and peered out. His bus hadn't come yet! Nyamu said the driver's schedule had changed—one of the downsides of door-to-door transportation. Given the delay, how would we move David's belongings in time to pick him up from his day program in Hillsboro by 3:30?

While Phil and I waited outside the house, Nyamu returned to his duties. Medhanie said he sympathized with David because as a young person he had to leave his home in Eritrea very suddenly when his brother was killed during a political uprising, and his mother feared for the rest of the family. I remembered a similar story from a woman who had fled Cambodia in the middle of the night when she was a child and still mourned the loss of her pet chickens. Though David's situation was different, a sudden separation from familiar surroundings could be traumatizing for him, too.

A half-hour later, David's small Tri-Met bus pulled into the driveway and he climbed inside. We descended on his room, dismantled his bed, removed the drawers filled with clothes from his tall chest, and scooped the Disney books and figurines from his book case. I grabbed his clothes, still on their hangers, from his closet and carried them to the back seat of our Subaru. I removed David's picture of the Native American woman and her infant and his case of Special Olympics medals from his wall and took them to the Subaru. Everything else went in the back of Medhanie's red pickup.

Before we pulled out of the driveway, Nyamu said to Phil, "It just isn't right that David has to leave." As a staff member at 89th Court when David moved in, he'd known David during a more auspicious time, before changes in staff and housemates. He knew David didn't mean to be disruptive.

We followed Medhanie's red pickup through neighborhoods and main streets onto I-5. On the freeway, the blanket Medhanie had lodged between David's dresser and recliner to prevent them from rubbing together loosened and flapped in the wind. Phil tried to motion Medhanie to stop. Finally, the blanket blew onto the grass at the roadside. We kept driving.

After we got to Saint Helens, Medhanie, his wife, Saba, and a newly hired staff person, Sandra, helped us carry David's things into the house and place them in his bedroom. We pushed his extra-long, full-size bed against the wall to make more space in the small room, and Sandra helped me make the bed. I hung David's clothes in the closet and set his books and figurines on his book shelf for him to arrange. Finally, I propped the picture of the Indian woman and her baby on the book case to hang later above his bed.

When we finished, we had fifteen minutes before we needed to leave to pick up David. Saba prepared a chicken dish with a tantalizing spicy aroma, but we had no time to eat.

At David's day program, we repeated the same process we had gone through at the group home of saying goodbye to staff. Like Nyamu, they assured us they would miss David.

On the drive to his new home in Saint Helens, David was calmer than he'd been in weeks. "No more CITE," he said, referring to his day program. He sounded resigned. I'd asked the staff at his home and at the day program to try to prepare him for his move by talking about it whenever possible. They'd done a good job.

"Spend the night at Medhanie's," David said. At least, he understood that much. But did he think he was visiting Medhanie for a sleepover and would return to his home the next day? He looked inside the overnight bag I'd placed on the backseat next to him so he would have something to carry into the house—an object to mark his transition to a new home.

"No pajamas?" he asked. I'd been so caught up in the physical aspects of the move that I hadn't given much thought to what David would carry into the house. His overnight bag only reinforced the idea that he was going to Medhanie's for a short stay.

"You have pajamas at Medhanie's house," I said sheepishly, thinking of his possessions we had just moved. David accepted my explanation without further questions.

That evening, David, Phil, and I ate pizza with Medhanie, Sandra, and the other resident who would be David's housemate. Saba had gone home to fix dinner for the family's children in Portland. A few months earlier, Medhanie had rented this home to begin a new venture. He lived apart from his family to provide foster care in Saint Helens, where he'd found a client.

It was too soon to know how David's move would work out. We'd tried for three years to change David to fit his group home. We hoped this new home would fit *his* needs. We'd intervened in his life without his permission, but our actions had been done with love and concern for his wellbeing. We'd done our best, all we could do.

VI.

Two fish shine
below the surface,
an iridescence.

They glide through
rippling water
alone, together.

Phyllis Mannan

34

Swimming Our Own Way
Together but Apart

I awake remembering a dream filled with bright colors and a feeling of lightness. A few minutes later, I sit at the computer drinking Earl Grey tea, looking out at my sliver of the Pacific Ocean. Yellow-breasted finches flit in the wild huckleberry. Words flow easily. I'm coming closer to what I want to say . . .

Eighteen years ago, a young boy pointed out a torn fish in the dentist's office where I waited for David to have his teeth cleaned. After the boy left with his mother, I bent in front of the tank to look for the torn fish. I was repelled by what I found. A dead fish appeared to be two, trying to swim apart but held by a common tail. Though I fought the notion, the image later reminded me of my relationship with David: We were linked not only by blood, but by his dependence upon me for daily care.

In 1971, David was a newborn, the first grandchild on both sides of our family. The possibilities for his future and ours seemed limitless. Now, he's a forty-three-year-old, disabled man with aging parents. Not only does he have autism and significant intellectual impairment, but bipolar and obsessive-compulsive disorders have complicated his life.

In spite of these obvious challenges, I see growth in him and feel hope for his future. I'm confident that with the right living situation and support, he can surmount his problems. He's shown more resilience than I thought possible. In his twenties, he experienced the onset of mental illness. Yet, at age thirty, he moved with minimal difficulty from our family's home to a group home. In his late thirties, his bipolar disorder and OCD led to an emotional crisis, but he successfully transitioned from a group home to adult foster care. For the past year-and-a-half, he's been happy living with a single caregiver and with one housemate or, currently, none. He smiles and enjoys spending time with others. The facial twitches which developed during his years in the group home have completely disappeared.

These experiences show David needs the consistency of one central caregiver to feel safe. When he lived with Phil and me, I was his anchor. For a short time after his move to the group home, Jennifer, the program manager, played this role. Later, he lit up whenever he mentioned a young staff member who took him to church, restaurants, and movies. When she moved out of state, returned, and left again, he seemed distraught.

Nyamu became David's next anchor, though he worked only weekends at the group home and returned to Kenya to visit his family for six weeks each summer.

During one trip to Kenya, Nyamu contracted a virulent strain of malaria that took months to cure. As the time dragged on before he could return to work, David reassured himself, "Nyamu will come back, Nyamu will come back." He also remarked, "Nyamu is a good kind of guy," an unusual observation on his part. David's final years at the group home were marked by the program manager's extended medical leave, which left him without a central person he trusted and appeared to contribute to his decline.

Now, David depends upon his adult foster care provider for stability. If he weren't happy with his caregiver, our family would need to lend more support. Phil and I would have to attend countless meetings to search for solutions and receive troubling phone calls and incident reports, as we did during his final years in the group home.

The absence of such meetings and reports means David is doing well; he doesn't need us as much. Sometimes, though, I feel like a mother who has dropped off her child at school for the first time. She's happy he's moving ahead, beginning to have a life apart from her, but she also feels a part of her is missing. She's been concentrating so much time and energy on the child since his birth. Now, she must find a new focus for her energy.

Not only do I see growth in David, but I see growth in our family. Our understanding and acceptance of David and others with disabilities has expanded. We've learned there's more to a person than what he or she knows. If we can't connect with our mind, we connect with our heart. This ability enlarges our capacity to love.

After our family learned David was developmentally delayed, I wrote to my friend Lillian, the only person I knew who had a child with developmental disabilities. How could we help David? How could we accept our new role as the parents of a disabled child? My friend wrote back, "David will teach you." Her answer puzzled me. I couldn't imagine how he would teach us.

In the forty years since Lillian's counsel, David has grown from a blond toddler to a tall, brown-haired man. I've gone from a tall, brown-haired, young teacher to a slightly hunched, gray-haired retiree. During these years, I've learned some lessons about parenting—about life itself—and many of these lessons have come from David and our other two children.

First, I've learned the child has a right to simply *be*. In other words, parents need to love and accept their children as they are. It helps to remember that they're made up of more than their intellect, achievements, appearance, potential occupation, earning power, and possessions.

In keeping with this idea, parents of a disabled child—any child—should try to give up the idea their identity is closely linked to the child's. For years, I had a recurring dream of a beautiful boy or girl who sat on my lap and looked up at me, making me feel good. This offspring stood in opposition to the physically disabled, seizure-ridden children in other dreams. Apparently, I hadn't come to terms with having a child who didn't match my idea of perfection. After years of such dreams, I realized it's not the child's role to make the parent feel good; it's the child's role to simply *be*. The parent's role is to love the child.

When David was growing up and during his adult years before he moved to the group home, I placed too much importance on his appearance. Not only did I try to make sure he was clean and well groomed, but I tried to imprint on him my image of how he should look. If he let me, I parted his hair and combed it to the side. Sometimes, he took the comb afterward and brushed the hair over his forehead, the way he liked it. It was natural for me to want his appearance to reflect well on our family, but it was wrong to try to turn him into a person of my choosing. In effect, I was saying to him and to the world he wasn't good enough as he was.

Another thing I've learned is to be process-oriented rather than goal-oriented. Having a disabled child teaches one that success usually comes in small steps. A skill that would normally come in a relatively short time, like using the toilet or tying one's shoes, might take years to acquire—if it can be acquired at all. As every parent of a disabled child and special education teacher will tell you, the successes are sweet when they arrive.

Yes, David has taught me much: humility, patience, and the obvious truth that children teach their parents.

I think again of the cool candling room where Uncle Arthur taught me to hold an egg to the light to detect its purity. Trying to discern David's personhood—anyone's, for that matter—is like attempting to look into an opaque egg. Who is to say what each of us is or was meant to be? It's hard to know this about someone without an intellectual disability, partly because our place in the world isn't fixed throughout our lives. Much about autism and mental illness is unknowable; we grope for answers and can't find them. But in the process of searching, we find strength. In addition, the search binds us with others seeking answers.

Nothing prepared me for having a child with a disability. Not education, not religious faith, not a happy childhood. When David was young, Phil and I had no guidebook for raising him. I was unrealistic in my goals. My wish for David—for our whole family— was similar to what I looked for in the candled egg: perfection. If I couldn't have that, I'd settle for another nebulous state: normalcy. Though I still sometimes wish for those things, I know they don't exist, not for us, or for anyone. Now, my vision for David and each person in our family is simply to be moving toward wholeness.

In the years since my encounter with the torn fish, I've realized David and I are bound by family ties, love, and experience—and, to some degree, by his disability—but this connection is not unyielding. Our bond allows us to be ourselves, to swim separately. If

David could speak for himself, I think he would say, "We are two fish, swimming our own way."

When Phil and I visited David in January 2014, he smiled when we left and said, "Shake your hand?" I took his hand, grateful for the connection. I remembered that after my return from a week-long writers' conference sixteen years earlier, David had restored the clock radio to my nightstand and urged me to pull the minivan into the garage, anxious to return things to their proper places, but hadn't said a word of welcome or showed he cared I was home. His handshake now could not have meant more.

David will always need our advocacy and support. He will need family members and caregivers to act as his interpreters, to listen to him and try to read his preferences. Yet, he is also his own person. He will help to shape his life. To the extent possible, he will write his own narrative.

NOTES

According to the U.S. Centers for Disease Control and Prevention, about one in 68 children in the United States has been identified with an Autism Spectrum Disorder. The condition is from four to five times more common in boys than in girls. An estimated one out of 42 boys and one in 189 girls is currently diagnosed with autism in the United States—a ten-fold increase since David was born in 1971.
"Data &Statistics," Centers for Disease Control and Prevention, last modified March 14, 2014,
http://www.cdc.gov/ncbddd/autism/data.html

There is a great deal of evidence that most autism is caused by changes, or mutations, in genes. Since the mapping of the human genome in 2000, scientists have identified many gene patterns associated with autism, but they still don't have a clear picture of the causes. The current theory is that genetic factors predispose a person to develop autism, but environmental factors also play a role.

Chapter 2: The Small White Spot—David's Birth and Diagnosis

Today, researchers recognize one of the earliest signs of autism is that the toddler shows little sign of trying to attract the attention of another person by look or gesture. Most normally developing babies point to an object with a finger by eighteen months. David didn't do this. What's more, he didn't look at an object someone else pointed to or try to follow their gaze. Even now, no amount of insisting or cajoling can get him to look at an object. Joint attention isn't a trait he can acquire. Something is at fault in the part of his brain researchers call *the social brain*—the part that makes eye contact and joint attention possible.

Uta Frith, *Autism: A Very Short Introduction* (New York: Oxford University Press, 2008), 18-19, 72-73.

Chapter 6: Running that Track Forever—The School Years

1. "What is IDEA?," National Center for Learning Disabilities, accessed January 23, 2015, http://www.ncld.org/disability-advocacy/learn-ld-laws/idea/what-is-idea

2. "Definition of 'intellectual disability,'" American Association on Intellectual and Developmental Disabilities, accessed January 23, 2015, http://aaidd/intellectual-disabilitiy/definition

3. Autism Speaks, accessed January 23, 2015, http://www.autismspeaks.org/what-autism

Chapter 7: Ghosts at Tryon Creek—Sensory Perception and Self-Awareness

In *Without Reason: A Family Copes with Two Generations of Autism* (New York: Signet, 1989), Charles Hart reports that his son Ted also tore the edges of pictures he liked: "Sometimes part of the page was missing. Elsewhere the rip was no more than a tentative little tear or notch at the border of the page, as if he had wanted only a scrap of paper to associate with a favorite image, but was afraid to remove the entire picture." (108)

Alvaro Pascual-Leone asserts people with autism "lack an emotional response to self." Using a magnetic wand to briefly interrupt brain function, Pascual-Leone and his colleagues determined the right side of the brain, behind the forehead and temple, is critical for knowing one's own emotions.
William J. Cromie, "Scientists look people in the 'I': Best Place to locate the 'self' is in the brain," Harvard University Gazette (April 12, 2001), httpwww.news.harvard.edu/gazette/2001/04.12/01-selfawareness.html

4. Temple Grandin, *Thinking in Pictures: And Other Reports from My Life with Autism* (New York: Vintage Books, 1995), 62-81.

5. Richard Restak, M.D., *The Brain Has a Mind of Its Own: Insights from a Practicing Neurologist* (New York: Harmony Books, 1991), Uncorrected Proof, 150.

6. Patricia Stacey, *The Boy Who Loved Windows: Opening the Heart and Mind of a Child Threatened with Autism* (U.S.: Da Capo Press, 2004), 146-147.

Chapter 9: What Are People For?—Problems Relating to Others

Scientists use the term "theory of mind" to describe the ability to understand that other people have thoughts and impulses that are different from one's own. People with autism often lack this ability; they find it difficult, if not impossible, to put themselves in another person's place. (Frith, 67-72.)

7. Judy Barron and Sean Barron, *There's a Boy in Here: Emerging from the Bonds of Autism,* (Texas: Future Horizons, 1992), 20-21.

Chapter 10: A Tale of Two Brothers—Using Ritual to Deal with Change

8. Grandin, 34-37.

Chapter 11: Echolalia in Green—The Diagnosis of Bipolar and Obsessive-Compulsive Disorders

9. Grandin, 54.

10. Eleanor Roosevelt, "Where Do Human Rights Begin?," *Courage in a Dangerous World: The Political Writings of Eleanor Roosevelt,* ed. Allida M. Black (New York: Columbia University Press, 1999), 190.

Chapter 27: Making Things Happen—Advocating for Health Care and Daily Support

11. Chris Krenk, "In My Opinion: When Medicine Hurts," *The Oregonian,* February 16, 2002.

12. Alan Lytle, Oregon Technical Assistance Corporation, *2007 ISP Handbook: A guide to Individual Support Planning for families, friends and guardians of people supported in Oregon,* Version 2.0 DRAFT, September 2007.

Chapter 29: Frizzled—Anxiety, OCD, and Separation from Self

13. Christine T. Wong et al, "Cell Communication and Signaling," 2014, http://www.biosignaling.com/content/12/1/19

14. U.S. National Library of Medicine, 2011, http://www.ncbi.nlm.gov/pubmedhealth

15. Frith, 23.

Chapter 33: The End Waves at You from the Beginning—The Move from 89th Court

16. Oregon Department of Human Resources, "Developmental Disabilities Administrative Rules," December 28, 2014, www.dhs.state.or.us/policy/spd/alpha.htm

BIBLIOGRAPHY

The following books are either cited in *Torn Fish*, or informed the writing.

Ackerman, Diane. *A Natural History of the Senses.* New York: Vintage Books, 1990.

Barron, Judy and Sean Barron. *There's a Boy in Here: Emerging from the Bonds of Autism.* Texas: Future Horizons, 1992.

Buscaglia, Leo F., Ph.D. *Personhood: The Art of Being Fully Human.* New York: Fawcett. Columbine, 1978.

Collins, Paul. *Not Even Wrong: Adventures in Autism.* New York: Bloomsbury, 2004.

Finland, Glen. *Next Stop: An Autistic Son Grows Up.* New York: Berkley Books, 2012.

Frith, Uta. *Autism: A Very Short Introduction.* New York: Oxford, 2008.

Garvin, Eileen. *How to Be a Sister: A Love Story with a Twist of Autism.* New York: The Experiment, 2010.

Grandin, Temple. *Thinking in Pictures: And Other Reports from My Life with Autism.* New York: Vintage Books, 1995.

Greenfeld, Karl Taro. *Boy Alone: A Brother's Memoir of Growing Up with an Autistic Sibling.* New York: Harper Perennial, 2009.

Hart, Charles. *Without Reason: A Family Copes with Two Generations of Autism.* New York: Signet, 1989.

Karasik, Paul and Judy Karasik. *The Ride Together: A Brother and Sister's Memoir of Autism in the Family.* New York: Washington Square Press, 2003.

Restak, Richard, M.D. *The Brain Has a Mind of Its Own: Insights from a Practicing Neurologist.* New York: Harmony Books, 1991.

Robinson, John Elder. *Look Me in the Eye: My Life with Asperger's.* New York: Three Rivers Press, 2007.

Stacey, Patricia. *The Boy Who Loved Windows: Opening the Heart and Mind of a Child Threatened with Autism.* U.S.: Da Capo Press, 2004.

ACKNOWLEDGMENTS

This book is dedicated to my family: to David, who has shown great courage in his forty-three years; to my husband, Phil, who has been beside me in every struggle and triumph; to Jon and Lisa, who allowed me to share their stories whenever they intersected with David's; and to my mother, Geraldine Meyers, who has been a steady beacon throughout my life and a best friend to David. I also thank my brothers, Mark and Tim Meyers, and my sister, Christine Snodgrass, who have given their unconditional love and support.

My great appreciation goes to poetry writing teachers and mentors John Brehm, Nance Van Winckel, and Christopher Howell, who deepened my understanding of imagery and compressed language. When I began writing narrative nonfiction, the late Michael Burgess offered invaluable editing advice and encouragement.

Many thanks to Debra Brimacombe, Perri Gaittens, Tela Skinner, Robin Reid, Gail Balden, Julianne Parrett, Elizabeth Bristol, Kay Stolz, and other fellow writers who have offered helpful suggestions and faithful support.

Thank you also to my editor, Marcia Silver, and to agent Holly Lorincz.

Phyllis Mannan is a champion for her son and others with developmental disabilities. She served on the board of directors of Edwards Center and Bethesda Lutheran Communities Family Association. Her nonfiction stories and poems appear in northwest literary magazines. A former high school English teacher, she lives with her husband on the north Oregon coast.